Par

- TOYS & GAMES • BOOKS
- HOME VIDEO • AUDIO CASSETTES
- COMPUTER PROGRAMS
- MAGAZINES

Parents' Choice

A Sourcebook of the Very Best Products to Educate, Inform, and Entertain Children of All Ages

SELECTED BY DIANA HUSS GREEN
FOUNDER AND EDITOR, *PARENTS'
CHOICE* MAGAZINE

ANDREWS AND McMEEL

A Universal Press Syndicate Company
Kansas City

Library of Congress Cataloging-in-Publication Data

Green, Diana Huss.
    Parents' choice : a sourcebook of the very best products to
  educate, inform, and entertain children of all ages / selected by
  Diana Huss Green.
      p. cm.
  Includes bibliographical references and indexes.
  ISBN 0-8362-8036-9 : $9.95
    1. Toys—Catalogs. 2. Bibliography—Best books—Children's
  literature. 3. Children's literature—Bibliography. 4. Audio-
  visual materials—Catalogs. 5. Computer programs—Catalogs.
  I. Title.
  GV1218.5.G7   1993   93–5324
  790.1'33'0216—dc20   CIP

For David McCord

Contents

Preface

FOR CHILDREN, as for adults, excellence requires arduous effort. Curiosity, good manners, irreverence, the pride of discovery, objectivity, brazenness, passion, and self-doubt in unequal but balanced amounts have always contributed to achievement. Achievement is accompanied by self-esteem.

We have compiled for children a group of tools that may help them accomplish both. These tools—toys, books, videos, audios, magazines, computer programs—have been selected to help them also learn flexibility and rules to better understand and enjoy life. Here is a core extracurriculum of material to nourish the first generation of young adults who will enter the twenty-first century—to inform their minds, starch their characters, and open their hearts.

While we wait and work for improved public education, mothers and fathers are on their own. It is our informed guess that the family, with the help of grandparents, aunts, uncles, day-care moms, teachers, and librarians, can enrich, if not supplant, public schools.

It will not be easy but, for now, it's essential.

Beyond reading aloud to children early and often, there are letters and numbers to teach. The right TV and home video programs will help. There are toys that prompt youngsters to teach themselves. There are good audio cassettes for listening to and learning from. Computer programs can effectively involve even a two-year-old. Available, too, are good new books and good old ones. All these categories span ages and stages from babyhood to young adulthood.

Never before have we had so much fine material to buy or borrow and never before has it been harder to make choices. Needed time and information are tough to come by. The purpose of this book is to provide the latter and save the former.

What Is Parents' Choice?

Parents' Choice Foundation, a nonprofit service organization, was founded in Newton, Massachusetts, in March 1978 to offer families information to help their children learn.

Parents' Choice is funded in part by individual and corporate grants. Money is also raised through projects such as the _Parents' Choice Guide to Video Cassettes for Children,_ a Consumers' Report Book, and the sale of this book. But the lifeblood of Parents' Choice flows from the work of volunteers across the country. They make the following efforts possible:

A quarterly called _Parents' Choice,_ which remains the country's only nonprofit consumer guide to children's books, videos, toys and games, computer programs, recordings, magazines, movies, and television.

What-Kids-Who-Don't-Like-to-Read-Like-to-Read, a compilation of children's books for reluctant readers. Initiated in 1983, the book list has been offered on TV and radio by many stars such as LeVar Burton, Tony Randall, Howard Rollins, Jr., Rita Moreno, and Bob Newhart, as well as the late Lucille Ball and Sammy Davis, Jr.

Read-to-Achieve, a program that brings children's books to schools and libraries in the most deprived areas of major cities across the country. It, too, offers a free book list through the volunteered talent of show business personalities: Susan Saint James, Susan Lucci, Ed Asner, Charles Durning, Shari Lewis, Willard Scott ("Today Show"), Joel Seigel ("Good Morning America"), and Yogi Bear are among them.

And Parents' Choice Awards, established in 1980, which have been identifying for parents the year's best in all the media for children of different ages, backgrounds, skills, and interests. The awards are announced on national television shows such as "Good Morning America," "Today Show," "Entertainment Tonight," and "CBS Morning News" and reported in nearly four hundred newspapers, including _USA Today,_ the _Los Angeles Times,_ the _Chicago Sun-Times,_ the _Boston Globe,_ the _San Francisco Chronicle,_ the _New York Daily News,_ and the _Wall Street Journal. TV Guide, Woman's Day, Ladies' Home Journal,_ and _Family Circle_ are among the magazines that have noted them.

Some People Involved

Selection of the awards comes from the donated time of many prominent journalists, educators, artists, critics, publishers, storytellers, computer and other scientists, business people, musicians, and filmmakers. Most are parents, grandparents, or godparents working in New York, Los Angeles, Chicago, Atlanta, Albuquerque, St. Paul, and other cities; all search for the best with fine-toothed combs.

Among our judges are William A. Henry III, _Time_ magazine; Diane Roback, _Publishers Weekly;_ Joan Lunden, "Good Morning America"; Susan

Roman, American Library Association Services to Children; Trevlyn Jones, *School Library Journal;* Barbara Elleman, Book Links; Mary Ellen Quinn, director of collection development, Chicago Public Library; Eda White, Los Angeles Public Library; Marylyn Berg Iarusso, New York Public Library; Malcolm Charles Green, National Association of Theatre Owners; David Bianculli, New York TV critic; Charles Champlin, critic-at-large; Lee Margulies, *Los Angeles Times;* Ed Siegel, John Koch, *Boston Globe;* Pat Murphy, *TV Guide;* John Voorhees, *Seattle Times;* Noel Holston, *Minneapolis Star Tribune;* Ollie Reed, *Albuquerque Tribune;* Joe Stein, *San Diego Union Tribune;* Greg Dawson, *Orlando Sentinel;* Al Sanoff, *US News & World Report;* Brian Donlon and Matt Rousch, *USA Today.*

Others who serve in every area are children themselves. They are kids who go to preschool, child-care, schools, or camps in the inner city or suburbs of Atlanta, Boston, Chicago, New York, Los Angeles, or Washington, D.C.

All their work, adults' and children's, springs from their ongoing community spirit and their unfailing sense of fun.

ACKNOWLEDGMENTS

Researchers, Writers, and Responsibility

Among those whose distinguished long-term and generous work for Parents' Choice is the basis of the research, writing, and judgments here are: Kemie Nix, 1993 member of the Newbury selection committee; nationally acclaimed toy expert Ruth B. Roufberg; American Library Association's audio and video recording specialists Kristi Beavin, Erika Stokes, Laurie Tynan, Irene Wood; *Video Librarian's* Randy Pitman; children's book artists Marcia Sewall, Lydia Dabcovich, Marian Parry, Karen Ann Weinhaus, Ned Delaney, Ed Emberly, Marylin Hafner; computer specialists Cynthia Dye, Margaret Lurie, Stephen Perry; Professor of Library Science Selma Richardson; Susan Bloom, Simmon's Center for the Study of Children's Literature; librarians Susan Raskin, Phyllis Wiggin, Alice Stern, Miriam Temkin, Judy Matterazzo-Fagan; journalists Peter Neumeyer, Tanya Isch, Sandra Devaney, Susan Perry, Terri Payne Butler, Loretta McAlpine, Delia O'Hara, Mopsy Strange Kennedy. In addition, there is Elizabeth West, whose editorial and personal mind-set is consummately sensible, but always courageous. Each of these people (artists, academicians, researchers) is, as E. B. White's Wilbur said of Charlotte the Spider, "a good friend and a good writer."

Julia Cahill, valued Parents' Choice Foundation staff member, and Abigail Detweiler, assistant managing editor of *Parents' Choice,* provided research assistance. Elizabeth Carmichael supported them lavishly.

Maggie Russell, managing editor, made the book, as she makes everything at Parents' Choice Foundation possible because her work is impeccable and delicate; her almost perfect kindness comes from a life of constant practice, and her humor is naughty.

Any errors here are mine.

DIANA HUSS GREEN

Where Is It?

In the Book . . .

Each item in each chapter is listed by title in Index I on p. 133.

In Index II all titles in all chapters are listed in age-appropriate groupings. For example, if you are looking for a video for a four-year-old, go to Index II, find Video, check the preschoolers' group and make your selections. Proceed the same way in Toys, Audio Recordings, and Computer Programs.

For books, the authors, illustrators, and editors are listed in Index III. Index IV lists composers and audio recording artists.

Every toy, book, video cassette, audio recording, and computer program reviewed here has a title, a publisher, or a manufacturer. All have a retail price and a suggested age. As noted, book information also includes authors or illustrators and an ISBN number for easy location in libraries.

Recommended items that are referred to only in the narratives within the chapters are also noted in the indexes.

In the Mall . . .

In case you can't easily find a product in your neighborhood stores we've provided company and catalog addresses and phone numbers. Call companies for stores closest to you or consider mail-order through catalogs. Please be aware that legitimate businesses sometimes change hands and addresses with little notice, so call before you place an order or send a check.

Keep written records of all orders made by mail or phone. In case of any problems you will be on solid ground.

Toys

FANTASTIC TOYS don't just captivate. They help shape lifelong interests, lead to careers, focus passions. Have you ever wondered what early mechanical experiences led to Wilbur and Orville Wright's accomplishments? What hours of play and observation honed Thomas Edison? And which playthings shaped Amazing Grace Hopper (admiral, USN), Steven Jobs, Julia Child, Colin Powell, Sally Ride, Toni Morrison, Steven Spielberg, Connie Chung, Cher?

My Little Pony, G.I. Joe, and Strawberry Shortcake seem unlikely possibilities. More likely? A ball, crayons, Legos or Tinkertoys, a deck of cards, blank paper. For today's children, add access to a computer and some other modern magic.

It's the magic that's key. All toys worth their salt have it. They strike flint in the child's mind; they ignite imagination, stimulate creativity, elicit striving, and provoke the desire to make order. They whet and saturate appetites. They push, pull, and comfort. They help a child build a sense of self, a sense of ability to accomplish.

Toys offer children a first chance at providing *themselves* with a body of knowledge. Many children will root their imaginative life and internalize physical laws in that knowledge.

What Good Toys Are Not

Good toys are not instant gratification. They are not fast highs and quick crashes—they have staying power; they engage. They help build attention spans, not fragment them.

They do not excite interminable materialism. Required add-ons are rare in good toys.

Good toys do not glamorize or reflect the destructive aspects of society. A good toy does not offer answers; it stimulates questions and presents problems for solving—all in good humor. Sometimes with wit.

Try the following:

Rattles, Mirrors, and Musical Mobiles

Rattles too big to swallow, baby mirrors, and, if you like them, musical mobiles securely attached to the crib and well out of baby's reach are, along with a few stuffed animals, fine first toys. More and more handsome designs come in black and white because infants can't discern colors. As visual perception develops, red and other primary colors slowly come clear. Before their first birthdays most babies don't see pastels.

Double Feature (Wimmer-Ferguson) is a good crib mirror decorated in black and white. **Clutch Mirror** and **Baby Mirror** are handheld non-glass items. The first is available from Beckley Cardy catalog and the second from Lakeshore.

Rattles abound. Some good ones are **Spinning Rattle** (T. C. Timber), **Shiny Rattle Assortment** (Fisher-Price), and **Twin Rattle Teether** (Growing Child).

Dakin's **Circus Musical Mobile,** which plays "Rock-a-Bye Baby," dangles five different plush animals. Each pet detaches for separate play as the child grows. **Domino Babies Musical Mobile** (Dakin) is aesthetically quite appealing—all its animals are black and white panda bears—but as the animals are all the same, future play will be limited.

Avoid musical mobiles if you believe the crib should be associated with sleep, not with activity. Some feel an awake baby uses toys best in an infant seat. The **Tot Mobile** (Tot) hung nearby is an extraordinary example of excellence in design and practicality.

Among other time-tested toys for infants and toddlers are:

Skwish Classic
Pappa Geppetto's Toys. $7.   *Ages 3 mo–3 yrs.*

Little ones are fascinated with the brightly colored nontoxic beads that slide easily back and forth as the child moves them. In addition, shiny bells

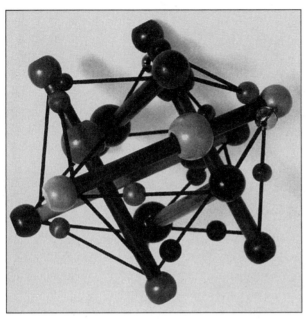

Skwish Classic

provide a pleasant sound in response to baby's touch. Suitably named, this toy "skwishes flat and bounces back."

Rock-a-Stack
Fisher-Price. $4.   *Ages 9 mo–3 yrs.*

Babies will grasp, bang, and teethe on the five brightly colored "dough-nuts" that fit onto a tapered post. Toddlers will enjoy the challenge of stacking the rings in order of size or color and will delight in unscrewing the post, then replacing it on the rocking base.

Little Red Ride-On
Fisher-Price. $25.99.   *Ages 9 mo–3 yrs.*

When its handle is locked into the upright position this toy is a walker; when the handle is released, it's a wagon; when the lift-up seat is opened, it's a hidden storage compartment—the perfect place for storing small items like blocks or tops.

Bag 'n' Train
Century Products. $38.   *Ages 1–3.*

Three soft-sculpted square totes of red, yellow, and blue attach with Velcro,

Little Red Ride-On

Bag 'n' Train

both to wheels and to each other, forming a colorful pull-along train. The totes themselves can hold teddy bears or blocks while pockets provide storage for smaller possessions. Plenty of flaps, textures, and bright appliqués add visual and tactile appeal, and the totes nest for storage.

Neat New Toy

Kinderworks. $69.00–89.95.   *Ages 1–5.*

Children are drawn in by the sight and sound of this unique push toy, which consists of precision-cut hardwood dowels and beads, painted and polished to perfection and arranged in a complex pattern that looks some-

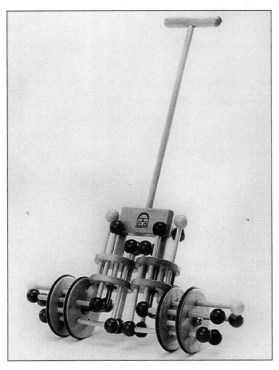

Neat New Toy

thing like a lawn mower. As the child pushes, rubber-cushioned wheels power the colorful rods, which ride up and down and around and around like carousel horses. As they move, marbles encased in the gears provide a satisfying clatter.

Fuzzy Puzzle
Lights, Camera, Interaction! $10.95.   *Ages 1–3.*

Framed as a puzzle, this variation on the cozy old book *Pat the Bunny* has a cow, a pig, a sheep, and a little chick. Each wears a textured, touchable coat, and each has a knob for tiny fingers to grasp. Children will pat and befriend the animals. Each is big enough to help train little hands to aim, position, and finally manipulate the animal back into its self-shaped spot.

Baby's First Train
T. C. Timber. $29.95.   *Ages 18 mo–3 yrs.*

Nine finely polished wood pieces in shining primary colors come easily apart and together to make a handsome and well-crafted train that appeals

Baby's First
Train

to all the senses. Colored sorting pegs encourage manipulation while helping a baby develop a sense of different sizes. The mirror and squeaker stimulate more robust actions and reactions.

Blocks

Among the world's best toys, blocks stimulate imagination, provoke and satisfy curiosity, and are a cornerstone for learning aspects of math, physics, creativity, spatial relations, and more. Besides—they are fun. So, if you plan to invest in a set beyond the soft fabric "baby" blocks, do your homework. Check some school supply catalogues or teachers' stores. Both sell the classic hardwood unit building blocks, which are best of all. T. C. Timber is a company that offers fine wooden sets through regular stores. **Dr. Drew's Discovery Blocks** are worthy too. **Lotsa Blocks** is an alternative.

Building Sets

Another group of toys so cherished and well used by children that many companies produce them includes the internationally lauded Lego. Begin with their **Duplo Building Sets** for one-and-one-half- to five-year-olds. Then it's on to the fine and full **Lego Basic Build 'n' Store Chest.** Should you have a budding architect at your house, this company and others are well prepared with elaborate challenges for her or him.

A Canadian company, Ritvik, is less known but competitive in quality and price. Its **Mega Blocks 40 Piece Basic** is outstanding—its pieces are interchangeable with Lego sets. The entire range of **Erector** sets (Meccano) is respected, well loved, and superb. All three companies produce "systems," kits which are nearly impossible to differentiate in merit and quality. The basic **BRIO-Mec** sets are well designed, endlessly fascinating, and as tidy as any others. Shop for price.

If your kids want something store-bought and sassy, check these out:

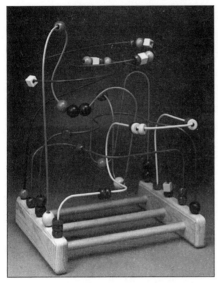

Original Rollercoaster

Original Rollercoaster
Anatex Enterprises. $49.95. *Ages 2–5.*

With its multicolored swoops and dips, this toy inspires the same finger-fiddling that an abacus invites. Each length of colored metal is bent into a different pattern and each is threaded with variously shaped bright beads. Children slide the beads along each wire, following its twists and turns, dips and rises, from end to end. The toy provides absorbing fun at the same time it challenges a child perceptually, physically, and mentally.

Folktails: Ladybug Puppet
Folkmanis. $16. *Ages 3–up.*

Children have always loved real ladybugs and they will be mesmerized by

Folktails: Ladybug Puppet

these black and red ones, fashioned handsomely out of a sturdy velvetlike material. The puppet slides onto the child puppeteer's hand like an over-size glove with one extra finger. The longest of little fingers can slide inside and work the puppet in appealing ways.

Toddler Tractor and Cart
Little Tikes. $30.   *Ages 18 mo–3 yrs.*

With this good-looking green plastic scoot-along vehicle and its detach-able yellow wheelbarrow, toddlers will enjoy such chores as hauling leaves and collecting sandbox toys for jaunts to the playground. Oversize tires and a fitted seat provide a secure perch, while the large steering wheel and assertive horn imitate those on a real tractor.

Activity Walker
Fisher-Price. $29.95.   *Ages 6 mo–3 yrs.*

This three-way contraption starts as a floor toy, one that has dials and flippers to manipulate. Then, as the baby becomes a toddler, the toy can become a stable walker. Ultimately, it converts to a play cart.

Spring-a-Ling
Educo International. $15.   *Ages 6 mo–3 yrs.*

Toddlers are fascinated with this springy, three-dimensional wire and bead

Activity Walker

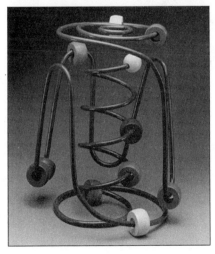

Spring-a-Ling

maze. As they twist and turn it, they send one to ten multicolored wooden beads careening around the continuous length of blue wire, which has been bent in such a complex shape that it seems soft, not rigid. Small, safe, and portable, Spring-a-Ling can easily accompany and amuse a restless child in a stroller or car.

1-2-3 Bike

Playskool. $34.99.   *Ages 2–5.*

With its unique three-stage wheel system, this bike can take a child from foot pushing to two-wheel pedaling. The secret is in two L-shaped brackets on which training wheels are mounted. Turn the brackets one way and the training wheels are wide apart, with the stability of a tricycle. Turn again and the wheels become standard training wheels. When the child is sufficiently skilled, remove the brackets entirely. And cheer.

Unicef Dolls

Unicef Dolls

European Toy Collection. $16.95 each.   *Ages 3–8.*

Children can't wait to get their hands on these multiheritage rag dolls, each dressed in a bright nation-announcing costume. The dolls are unified by their size and cheerful expressions, and each can wear the outfits of the others. Every doll—from the USA, Russia, China, Mexico, Great Britain, and Tanzania—comes with an illustrated booklet describing the customs, values, language, and exciting features of its country.

Art Supplies

As children become interested in learning arts and crafts techniques they are generally best off with materials that encourage their imaginations. Art stores, office supply outlets, and school supply houses often offer higher-quality paints, brushes, paper, etc., at more reasonable prices than do chain or discount stores. We suggest:

Paints

Powdered tempera paint lasts indefinitely; it can be mixed with water as needed to provide thick nondrip colors or thinner washes for watercolors. Liquid tempera is the easiest to use; just pour three (red, yellow, blue) or more colors into a muffin tin. **Tempera Blocks** are two-and-one-half-inch-diameter discs of compressed paint. They may come packed six or eight to a tray. Use with a thick brush and clean with a quick motion under a running faucet. **Non-Spill Paint Cups** have two caps. One has a hole just big enough to hold the paint brush; as long as the cup is less than half-full of paint, it cannot run out even if the paint cup tips over. A second cap snaps on top (after the brush is removed) to keep the paint from drying out between painting sessions. These come with color-coded caps to match the paints within. (*Tempera Blocks* and *Paint Cups* are available from *Toys to Grow On* catalog.) **Clean Colors/Washable Paint** from Marlon is a thick paint that won't drip. It does wash out of fabrics and off of walls.

Brushes

Thick round brushes with short, stubby handles give children good control. These are available with color-coded handles. Keep the same color brush in the matching paint cup, and change brushes each time you paint with a different color.

The best ready-made collection of paint supplies is the **Whole Rainbow Paint Center** from the *Toys to Grow On* catalog.

Paper

Newsprint, preferably 18″ x 24″, is inexpensive and satisfying; sometimes newspaper or printing plants give away ends of paper rolls. The unprinted sides of any large sheets, shirt cardboards, old newspapers, used magazines, or junk mail are usable caches for cutting, pasting, creating. They also introduce or reinforce a concept of thrift.

Easels

Tyke Easel ($100, Tyke) or similar school-style easels help children take their own work pridefully. Growing Child also sells a fine **Easel** ($58); it includes a chalkboard and a surface for wipe-off crayons or dry-erase markers. Little Tikes has a **Double Easel with Chalkboard** (about $55). The Fisher-Price unit, **Easel Desk** ($55), is an easel on one side and a sit-down desk on the other.

Dress-up

Old and glittery clothes from the backs of closets, yard sales, or really thrifty thriftshops are the basics. Add a few new ones—
Paraphernalia for Pretending, as well as the individual **Let's Pretend** kits from Creativity for Kids, offers some grown-up dress-up at often reasonable prices. **Grandma's Dress-up Trunk** (Toys to Grow On) is a 10-piece set for girls. The analogous **Grandpa's Dress-up Trunk** is also sold in the school catalog of the parent company (Lakeshore). Other Lakeshore fanciful clothes: **Around the World Hat Box, Make-Believe Hat Box, Career Hat Box, Great Adventures Trunk.**

In no way less creative or challenging but homing in on different talents are the following:

Learning Circles: Squares and Rectangles, Short and Tall Cylinders, Blocks and Triangles
Rhyme and Reason Toys. $29 each.   *Ages 3–6.*
These colorful wooden sets incorporate shape-fitting trays within the perimeter of a monorail track. A driver and flatbed vehicle slide around the track. The trays hold cubes and triangles, or squares and rectangles, or short and tall cylinders. Although each set is self-contained, children can combine the colorful pieces from different sets to make fanciful villages or abstract patterns.

Learning Circles

Sand and Water Activity Table

Playskool. $60. *Ages 2–7.*

A light but sturdy plastic table assembles in minutes and features two recessed areas with flip-top lids and built-in drain plugs for easy cleaning. Kids can make sand castles in one compartment and play with boats in the other. Hose everything down and the table is ready to use for artwork, board games, or picnics.

Puzzle Truck

Puzzle Truck

Heros/Darda. $37.95. *Ages 2–8.*

With its red hardwood cab, triple-sanded and super-lacquered, Puzzle Truck is so satisfying to the touch that kids will be tempted to take the pieces apart and put them back together again and again. The truck's cargo comprises brilliant red, yellow, blue, and green blocks that fit together into a neat puzzle. With cargo in place, the play truck can go tooting off, indoors or out, on nonmarring treaded rubber tires.

Activity Gym

Activity Gym
Little Tikes. $180.   *Ages 3–up.*

A four-paneled play environment, this one is sure to entertain and challenge children as they climb up onto its sturdy platform, slide smoothly down its slide, or crawl through its large holes to hide in or explore the inviting space below the platform. No hardware is necessary, because the smooth pieces slide and lock together. Corners are gently rounded, and all surfaces are easy to grab, hold, and use.

Dollhouses

A cardboard grocery store box painted in cheerful colors, turned on its side, and fitted with some small furniture can serve as home to a family of play people. Going a financial step higher you might try **Toddle Tots Family House** (Little Tikes, $12–$15). **1, 2, 3 Family House** (Playmobil USA, $61), one of the most attractive and practical of the plastic dollhouses, is available at most toy chains.

Wooden dollhouses, often more versatile, usually have more charm and usually cost more. There are exceptions. **My Little Home** (T. C. Timber, $42) provides construction-toy options to rearrange the living-space configurations. An open top offers access for floor play. **Community Builder** (Community Playthings) is a modular system of individual rooms that can be combined into one- or two-floor houses as well as into schools, garages, fire stations, etc. One spacious module is sixteen inches long, twelve inches deep, eight inches high; it costs about $30.00. A Masonite peaked roof is an additional $17.50. ABC School Supplies Inc. offers **Five Room Dollhouse** unfurnished for $59.95. Then there is, among others, the very nice **Ultra-Modern Dollhouse,** unfurnished for $109.95.

For older children seriously interested in this world of miniatures, assembling and collecting more elaborate dollhouses can become a lifelong hobby that is demanding, expensive, and satisfying.

Fairly priced toys that stimulate imaginative or academic play are sometimes inexpensive, but not always.

Chimalong
Woodstock Percussion. Junior/Deluxe, $30.00/49.50.   *Ages 3–up.*

Eight precision-tuned aluminum pipes are arranged in a foam-rubber holder. Children strike them with two rubber-tipped mallets, either picking out familiar melodies or just improvising. The accompanying songbook encourages players to match the different tubes with colors, numbers, and eventually musical notes. Happily, this instrument combines rich sound, a simple concept, and self-paced learning.

Big Dump Truck; Big Loader
Little Tikes. $23 each.   *Ages 3–up.*

These two sturdy yellow and black plastic vehicles may take care of a child's sandbox landscaping needs for years to come. About knee-high to a preschooler, the equipment is virtually indestructible, even by the elements. Both feature cabs that turn easily and move on large air-filled treaded tires. The lifting and hauling mechanics are just sophisticated enough to set scientifically inclined minds to wondering.

Poppets Doorway Theater
Poppets. $44.   *Ages 3–up (puppets not included).*

A red cloth panel hangs simply in a doorway. Behind the panel, children

Poppets Doorway Theater

hold hand puppets through the blue-striped flap that represents the curtain and the little stage. Below, blue-striped pockets can hold auxiliary actors (stuffed animals) or props. The theater is washable and easy to set up whenever someone shouts, "Let's put on a play!"

Hugg-a-Planet: Earth

Hugg-a-Planet. $19.95.   *Ages 9 mo–up.*

Hugg-a-Planet is a colorful stuffed globe covered in a soft but sturdy fabric that is patterned with a map of the earth. Children can play with it like a ball, study it like a map, and hug it like a friend. Its message—love our earth—was an early one in the spate of ecological toys.

Magiscope

Brock Optical. $125–$149.   *Ages 6–14.*

This sturdy microscope for children is unusual because it is an optically correct introduction to the real thing. The light source is available room light, so no lamps, mirrors, batteries, or cords are required. Several accessories, such as a Huygenian eyepiece with a magnification of ten or a fiber-optic acrylic rod for additional lighting, are fairly priced. Children can even carry this tool outside, since the Magiscope has no gear, racks, or threads that might be damaged by sand or water.

Creature Seeker

Uncle Milton Industries. $19. *Ages 6–10.*

Young explorers will relish and use all twelve pieces of this natural-science set, which allows them to uncover the creatures that live beneath their feet. The equipment includes a magnifying cylinder, a minimal micro-scope, identification chart, and stickers. Digging to examine earth's little creatures can be the precursor to a beginning respect for scientific method and for the intricacy of life.

Geosafari

Educational Insights. $99.95. *Ages 9–up.*

Geosafari uses computer technology and a game format to inspire children to learn geography. Avoiding both dreariness and gimmickry, it can be programmed for different ages and for children with different skills. Activities range from locating cities, countries, and landmarks to identifying world languages and currency. Other subjects include weather and explorations. Children will enjoy the space-age sounds and flashing lights as they play alone or with others.

Tensegritoy

Tensegrity. $30. *Ages 10–up.*

Budding architects, mathematicians, and engineers with perseverance and manual dexterity will enjoy this puzzle that challenges builders to discover nature's hidden patterns. Children, and probably many adults, will assemble wooden struts and elastics to form geodesic structures based on Buckminster Fuller's discoveries. Once assembled, the toy is a handsome hi-tech-looking kinetic sculpture that has both strength and bounce-ability.

Games

More and more games are becoming available for children two-and-a-half to three years old. They are valuable only if adults explain the rules

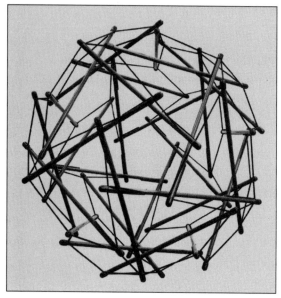
Tensegritoy

and play until little ones learn them. Then children can play with friends, practicing taking turns and other sociable skills. Remember, enjoying board games at any age is a matter of taste and disposition. For children three and up who've already shown such interest we suggest:

Snail's Pace Race
Ravensburger. $19.   *Ages 3–7.*

This charming color game for the very young requires no reading or number skills. Children roll colored dice to see which of the smoothly finished wooden snails will move closer to the finish line. The first snail to cross wins . . . but so does the last snail. In this satisfying situation for all, children practice color recognition and learn rudimentary game skills.

Music Maestro II
Aristoplay. $25.   *Ages 4–up.*

The game introduces the many sounds, shapes, and functions of forty-eight different instruments. It includes both a game board and two cassette tapes of instrument sounds made in classical, bluegrass, rock, and jazz ensembles. Five games of graduated difficulty provide fun and challenge beginning with very young music lovers.

Save the Forest

Battat. $15.99.   ***Ages 5–up.***

Children hear much about saving the environment, and this board game gives them some idea of what everyone is talking about. Players follow a path through the forest to discover animals and collect litter while learning respect for nature.

Don't Bug Me

Backos Game Company. $14.95. ·   ***Ages 6–up.***

This gardening game will have both parents and kids giggling. Each player is given a farmer and a bug. The object is to raise a variety of crops despite such random disasters as corn-ear worm or a neighbor's dog, and veggie-eating bugs that are always hungry. Bugs can be squashed, but they can recuperate in a "hospital" and return. The graphics are acceptable; the action is quick and hilarious.

In the Picture

Intempo Toys. $21.   ***Ages 6–up.***

A picture is missing from the main gallery of a museum. Is it a van Gogh, a Renoir, or the work of another famous artist? Players become both detectives and artists. They collect clues to identify the work, and then they race to put the missing picture back in the gallery. The game includes six reproductions of museum masterpieces and six of children's pictures; or players can create their own works.

Pictionary Junior

Games Gang. $14.   ***Ages 7–11.***

Clues to 480 possible words are given in pictures, and response time is limited, in this "charades on paper" game, which includes two wipe-off drawing boards, nontoxic crayons, and 120 cards.

Endangered

Family Games. $29.95.   ***Ages 8–up.***

Players undertake a world trek to search for twenty-four endangered animals and save them from extinction. Reason and Remedy cards reveal why they are endangered and what must be done to save them. Players must secure equipment, plane tickets, and vaccinations before they begin their journeys, and unexpected injuries or accidents can delay expeditions. Illustrations add to the appeal of this action-packed realistic game.

Huggermugger

Huggermugger
Western. $35. *Ages 8–up.*

This whimsically illustrated board game is (1) a treat for anyone with a literary bent and (2) a jog for those with limited vocabularies. Cards incorporate a choice of four challenges: scrambled words, multiple-choice definitions, spelling, and "Luck of the Draw." Players who answer correctly move around a grid featuring quaint pen-and-ink illustrations. They also get to peek at the letters hidden on the "Mystery Wheel," until they are able to decode the magic word and win.

Pyramids & Mummies
Aristoplay. $34. *Ages 8–up.*

This three-dimensional board game is totally engaging. Players first decipher cryptic messages to build a pyramid stone by stone. Then they enter passageways where the squares, like the die, are marked with hieroglyphs. While overcoming ancient curses and escaping from dangers, they learn to read pictographically. They also get an introduction to Egyptian gods. The first player to reach the Mummy Chamber wins. Even nonscholars will enjoy.

Pollution/Solution

Aristoplay. $20. *Ages 10–up.*

The game board is a map of a town. Players own real estate sections. Each area has a fifty–fifty chance of becoming either polluted or clean. When the pollution hits, it spreads randomly. Players learn solutions that stop the dangerous spread and protect everyone. Both chance and strategy play a part. The game is challenging, fun, and flexible.

Clever Endeavor

Western. $25. *Ages 12–up.*

Here is a trivia game with something extra—riddles and puns. Players get six hints (some of which are opaque) that should help to identify a person, place, thing, or event. Too many wrong guesses and you lose ground on the game board, but quick thinking ensures fast progress. For the most part, the material is clever, although some entries are silly. Since the game is invitingly open-ended, players can also come up with clue cards of their own.

Card Games

Great Women Series: Founders and Firsts, Foremothers, Poets and Writers

Aristoplay. $8 each. *Ages 10–up.*

Children's Authors Card Game

U.S. Games. $6. *Ages 7–up.*

Black History Playing Card Deck

U.S. Games. $8. *Ages 7–up.*

Inventors; Explorers; Scientists

U.S. Games. $5 each. *Ages 7–up.*

Fairytale Cards Series: Little Red Riding Hood, Puss in Boots, Sleeping Beauty, Cinderella

U.S. Games. $5 each. *Ages 5–up.*

Choosing Toys for Children

On the whole, a good toy:

- Can be played with in many ways.
- Challenges a child to do, think, or feel.
- Contributes to the development of a child's physical, mental, social, and emotional skills.
- Is attractive and well made, with pleasing shapes, colors, textures, or sounds.
- Is fun and fits a child's talents, interests, abilities, size.
- Fits in with your own tastes, knowledge, and pocketbook.
- Is safe.

Some rules for safety:

- A safe toy has no removable parts small enough to fit into a child's mouth. A rule of thumb—the smaller the child, the larger the toy's pieces should be.
- As soon as baby can reach high enough to get entangled, *remove* crib mobiles immediately.
- Outdoor toys that have wheels, runners, or gliders and are under three feet high should never be used without a supervising adult.
- Read labels to check for toxic paint or other material.
- Respect ages marked on toy boxes. While they may cover a wider age span than is realistic, they are there for your child's safety. After all, if a toy is not developmentally appropriate to your child, it is probably not safe for your child.
- The rules of safety are generally common sense rules—for example, a toy should be shatterproof, should be easily cleanable for health reasons.

Remember, if something seems dangerous, it probably is. Now, respect your instincts, your observations, and your child's interests.

2

Books

AS WE MOVE INTO the twenty-first century there is emerging a type of book collection no child should grow up without. The books in it tell the truth about the world, who is in it, what is in it, and what has always been in it.

The selections include fiction, nonfiction, and poetry. These books—here comes the nontraditional aspect—are competitive with the small screen. They must be as enticing as the tube, and by their nature, more enduring. They must capture and hold the child's attention through the authenticity, vigor, savvy, and glitz of their illustrations, characters, plot, or theme. They must speak to children in language children know, language they understand in their hearts. And the books must be funny because funny books make readers. They must be funny also because in an increasingly unfunny world, children need humor to build courage.

These are books that children read through to the end, *fast*. Then they read them again, though MTV blares and computer games beckon.

Most of the stories here are in English, some are in English and Spanish. A few in English originally come from an Asian language, and many are based in African folklore.

Women's literature is an integral part of these collections. And while some of the books are newly published, much of the literature is not new. As Alison Lurie says of folktales in *Don't Tell the Grown-ups*, "[They] portrayed a society in which women were as competent and active as men at every age and class. Gretel, not Hansel, defeated the witch and for every clever youngest son, there was a clever youngest daughter, equally resourceful" (Boston: Little, Brown, 1990).

Strong women take their place next to strong men in these books. Demagogues and dictators are part of it too. Sugar 'n' spice 'n' everything nice is just a portion of the most affecting children's literature. It always was.

If there is a unifying core of culture that exists for the world's children, it is the world's stories. The following books, which must be added to from time to time, are suggested to attract like the golden arches, to instruct as surely as the Parthenon's pillars, and to offer a common heritage to children from a diversity of backgrounds.

Nursery and Other Rhymes

Leaf through Lucy Cousins's illustrations in *The Little Dog Laughed* (Dutton) and you'll find you are laughing too. Bright balloon colors and childlike paintings reinterpret traditional rhymes and familiar words. Here little Miss Muffet is an African-American kid and so is Jill, who climbs the hill with Jack—he's still white. The king of Spain's daughter looks for all the world as if she were in a Mexico City school pageant. The crooked man who walks a crooked mile is clearly bent out of shape, and Mary, Mary Quite Contrary's garden grows a group of flowers with cheery multicultural children's faces.

In Chinese script, as well as in English, Robert Wyndham's *Chinese Mother Goose Rhymes* (Philomel Books) is gracefully and wittily illustrated by prize-winning artist Ed Young.

Moses Supposes His Toeses Are Roses
Retold and Illustrated by Nancy Patz. Harcourt Brace Jovanovich, ISBN 0-15-255-691. $4.95.

Dizzy McPeet, Sweetie McGuire, Betty Botter . . . it would be hard for a child to resist this rollick of eight less-than-familiar nursery rhymes. The exuberant two-color illustrations are inspired by Pennsylvania folk art but have a style of their own, full of flowing movement. Bonnets, shawls, pipe smoke, heads, and yes—toeses, float or burst from the frames on every page. A delight to read or chant to little ones.

Tortillitas Para Mama and Other Nursery Rhymes (Henry Holt) is a fine collection of Latin American rhymes and lullabies selected and translated by Margot Griego.

For traditionalists who love warm-spirited humor the *Random House Book of Mother Goose* brims with the late artist Arnold Lobel's impishness. *Nicola Bayley's Book of Nursery Rhymes* (Knopf), masterfully illustrated, is available in paperback for under $4.

As Dr. Seuss proved, singsong sounds, rhymes, and verse have ongoing appeal. None more than—

For Laughing Out Loud: Poems to Tickle Your Funnybone
Jack Prelutsky. Illustrated by Marjorie Priceman. Knopf,
ISBN 0-394-82144-0. $14.95. Read aloud.   *Ages 5–up.*

Here are 132 of the funniest poems ever assembled, filled with the sort of zany lunacy that makes kids giggle and parents groan before laughing. Children will cackle over the frogs that croak, the dog that brings in the mailman with the mail, and the little girl who learns how much easier life is when you're a slob. They'll laugh out loud at the boy who has a hot dog for a pet and at the captain who played the ukulele in his underpants.

Crazy to Be Alive in Such a Strange World, photographs by Alexander L. Crosby, (Evans) and *On City Streets* (Evans), both compiled by Nancy Larrick, are stunning examples of evocative read-aloud poems for children, parents, and grandparents of all backgrounds. Larrick offers tiny tangy tastes of poets such as John Ciardi, Langston Hughes, Shel Silverstein, Tennessee Williams, Erica Jong, Annie Dillard.

Water Pennies by N. M. Bodecker (McElderry Books) contains some of the finest fun in the language about nature's little creatures. The sound, if not the meaning, will make sense to the little ones, whose moms and dads can enjoy both right now.

There probably isn't a purist who, asked about the most highly regarded verse for children, wouldn't respond (and with some fanaticism) "Iona and Peter Opie's *Tail Feathers from Mother Goose*" (Little, Brown). But even they will chuckle, snicker, and giggle their way through *I Saw Esau* (Candlewick Press), Iona Opie's recent collaboration with Maurice Sendak. The modest editor herself calls the selections a "feast of laughter." She says "they have more oomph than zoom." It's true. Try stopping anywhere in the book. For example, on page 29:

> I was in the garden
> A-picking of the peas.
> I busted out a-laughing
> To hear the chickens sneeze.

Who could ask for more?

ABC Books

ABC books have come a long way. Preschoolers groove and grow with these delicate and meaty hors d'oeuvres.

C Is for Curious: An ABC of Feelings
Woodleigh Hubbard. Chronicle,
ISBN 0-87701-679-8. $12.95.   *Ages 2–5.*
Raging dragons, leaping cows, and baseball-playing dogs come together in this zany collection that explores every feeling from A(ngry) to Z(ealous). Children will delight in guessing each emotion and in letting their imaginations run free as they make up stories to go with each picture.

Alphabet Parade
Seymour Chwast. Gulliver/Harcourt Brace Jovanovich,
ISBN 0-15-200351-7. $13.95.   *Ages 2–5.*
The action begins right away, on the title page spread. The drum majorette leads off. A quick toss of her batons shapes the letter *A,* and the alphabet parade swings into motion. To our delight, we find an airplane, an alligator, an armadillo, an Arab, a man with an anchor, and a lady eating an apple. Turning the pages we see an amazing assortment of imaginative floats, each clearly defined and placed on a white background. Seymour Chwast has made an unlikely, hilarious game of "search for the letters" in his distinctly illustrated alphabet book. At the end, the crowd disperses, leaving letters to be swept up. A good time was had by all.

The Handmade Alphabet by Laura Rankin (Dial) presents the signing alphabet with astonishing clarity. *City Seen from A to Z* by Rachel Isadora (Greenwillow) is another way to look at the alphabet as well as at urban life. There are also *Peter Rabbit's ABC* (Penguin USA) using Beatrix Potter's illustrations and *ABC Animales* (Editoria Patria). *Ashanti to Zulu* by Margaret Musgrove with illustrations by Leo and Diane Dillon (Dial) has become a classic.

Satoshi Kitamura's *From Acorn to Zoo & Everything in Between in Alphabetical Order* (Farrar, Straus and Giroux) is newfangled fun— every person, animal, and object illustrated has a slightly quizzical expression and there's a bright off-center question on every page.

For older children who like a mystery with their art abecedarians, *The Z Was Zapped* by Chris Van Allsburg (Houghton Mifflin) will call them back again and again, even after they figure out the mysterious puzzle.

Counting Books

Simple, sassy, or scrumptious, one volume is more fascinating than the next. Know your child and make your choice. You won't go wrong with any of these.

When Sheep Cannot Sleep
Satoshi Kitamura. Farrar, Straus and Giroux,
ISBN 0-374-48359-0. $3.95. *Ages 3–5.*

No mere counting book, this is a work of art. Woolly, a sheep, cannot sleep. He goes for a walk in the meadow, and—incrementally—sees *one* butterfly, *two* ladybirds, *three* owls, and so on. He gets so tired he goes back home, lies down, thinks about all his *twenty-one* sheep sisters and brothers and uncles and aunts. Finally, he drops off, snoring (zzzzzzz) *twenty-two* z's. Kitamura's illustrations are startling in color, sophisticated, and enormously funny, as when Woolly stumbles into a house with thirteen doors, and once inside the house cooks himself sixteen peas.

Ten, Nine, Eight
Molly Bang. Puffin, ISBN 0-688-10480-0. $3.95.
Also available in hardcover. *Ages 2–4.*

A cozy countdown book that starts with ten small brown toes all washed and warm and nine soft friends in a quiet room. Children getting ready for bed will follow a daddy and a daughter through their reassuring nighttime ritual of hugs, kisses, and stuffed friends to tuck into bed. The lilting language and the softly colored pictures will help prepare little ones for their own bedtime rituals.

1, 2, 3 to the Zoo
Eric Carle. Philomel,
ISBN 0-399-21970-6. $5.95. *Ages 2–5.*

Modern as they look, Eric Carle's smashing book paintings have been bringing brilliant color to children's lives for many, many years. To learn about numbers and animals here is to have, as Mary Poppins would say, "a spoonful of sugar as the med'cine goes down."

Ten Little Rabbits
Virginia Grossman. Illustrated by Sylvia Long. Chronicle,
ISBN 0-87701-552-X. $12.95. *Ages 4–7.*

Classic counting rhymes take on new beauty as a warren of rabbits, clad in handwoven blankets, enact some of the traditional activities of North American Indians. These rabbits dance for rain, track animals through the woods, fish patiently with nets and spears, and flee a coming storm. The illustrations—detailed pen-and-ink drawings with striking watercolors in rich tones—depict the wide-open spaces of a rural landscape. The text's plain phrases effectively impart the values of native American culture. This handsome book has simplicity and quiet power.

One White Sail by S. T. Garne from Green Tiger Press, a Caribbean counting book, is unique as is artist–math teacher Teri Sloat's *From One to One Hundred* (Dutton).

Folk and Fairy Tales

In the best of all possible worlds every child would have a personal storyteller, an ancient and wise woman or man, thin as paper or fat as a berry, to say in soft, powerful tones how it was in the old days.

In this next best world we have writers and illustrators who tell these so-called grandmother stories. Their art nurtures our children's inner lives; it helps them know in their hearts, even before they know in their minds, the traditions and standards all people share.

Mufaro's Beautiful Daughters
John Steptoe. Lothrop, Lee and Shepard,
ISBN 0-688-04045-4. $13.   *Ages 5–8.*

Mufaro's daughters are indeed beautiful, but there the similarity between them ends. Nyasha is generous and good; Manyara is proud, vain, and selfish. When the Great King announces his desire for a wife, Mufaro plans to present both daughters as candidates. But Manyara is determined to be the Queen, and schemes to be first to appear before the King. As one might expect in folklore, her attitude brings about her downfall.

Inspired by an African folktale much like the European Cinderella, Steptoe tells this one with an original and graceful eloquence. Set near what is now Zimbabwe, the magnificent paintings breathe new life into traditional character types.

Goldilocks and the Three Bears
Retold and illustrated by Jan Brett. Putnam,
ISBN 0-399-22004-6. $5.95.   *Ages 5–8.*

Jan Brett is a storyteller in paint, who gives these three bears a life and history all their own. They live in a bear house designed just for them. It has a great wooden, carved bear bed featuring a headboard of bears ceremonially touching palms. In the margins is a veritable museum of a fairy-tale world, including mini-tales enacted by the book's characters or their friends. Endlessly interesting, this book tells many stories beyond Goldilocks's.

Eyes of the Dragon
Margaret Leaf. Illustrated by Ed Young. Lothrop, Lee and Shepard, ISBN 0-688-06155-9. $11.75. **Ages 6–9.**

According to thirteenth-century Chinese legend, if a dragon is painted on a wall it will fly off when its eyes are added. So-oo, when master artist Ch'en Jung agrees to draw a dragon on his town's wall he says he must do it his way or not at all. The town magistrate at first agrees, then breaks his word; he insists that Ch'en Jung add the eyes. The moment the eyes go on the dragon flies off, the wall crumbles, the sky fills with wrath. Illustrator Ed Young shows the story with brilliantly colored pastels in boldly designed pictures.

Iktomi and the Boulder
Retold and illustrated by Paul Goble. Orchard, ISBN 0-531-07023-9. $4.95. Also available in hardcover. **Ages 4–8.**

All solid citizens, particularly young ones, can instantly deduce that Iktomi is looking for mischief. He wasn't working, he wasn't helping his mother, he was walking along. . . . The tone of this Native American trickster tale is apparent from the first line. The mischievous, lazy, and legendary boy cavorts colorfully across the book's white pages and in and out of trouble. The illustrations, posterlike, are bold, handsome, and authentically painted by Paul Goble, who knows how to use white space better than anyone else.

Paul Bunyan
Retold and illustrated by Steven Kellogg. Mulberry/Morrow, ISBN 0-688-05800-0. $5.95. Also available in hardcover. **Ages 4–8.**

Steven Kellogg's hilarious version of the legendary Paul Bunyan story includes pictures teeming with people and animals embroiled in exaggerated activities. For example, Babe the Blue Ox reads a teeny book over the shoulder of a library patron. The illustrations drawn in fine and irresistibly funny lines are painted with gold-hued watercolors.

Baby Rattlesnake
Te Ata, Lynn Moroney. Illustrated by Mira Reisberg. Children's Book Press,
ISBN 0-89239-049-2. $13.95.   *Ages 4–8.*

Illustrated by striking full-color Santa Fe–style paintings, this Southwest
Native American tale tells a story of family love and forgiveness. Baby
Rattlesnake cries and cries for his own rattle. He finally receives one, even
though his parents think him too young. But he uses his new rattle to scare
small creatures. When he tries to scare the chief's daughter, she steps on
his precious rattle. Baby is devastated, but his family comforts him with
big rattlesnake hugs.

Sh-Ko and His Eight Wicked Brothers
Retold by Ashley Bryan. Illustrated by Fumio Yoshimura. Atheneum,
ISBN 0-689-31446-9. $12.98.   *Ages 4–8.*

As princesses go, Yakami is pretty perceptive. She is courted, but not fooled,
by Sh-ko's eight wicked brothers. Although he wants to court Yakami, Sh-ko
can't. He is straggling and struggling far behind his brothers, burdened by
their bags and baggage. He is also understandably distracted by an encounter with a naked rabbit. Ashley Bryan's engaging words and Fumio Yoshimura's flowing brushstrokes will enable even the youngest to enter into
the Japanese ambiance and humor of this tale.

The Story of Chicken Licken
Jan Ormerod. Lothrop, Lee and Shepard,
ISBN 0-688-06058-7. $13.   *Ages 2–6.*

This classic children's tale is presented here as a play. On the opening
pages the cast is silhouetted against a deep cerulean blue, which gives a
sense of "lights out" and the anticipation of things to come. Then two
stories unfold: that of Chicken Licken on the well-lighted stage, performed
by children in hilariously imaginative costumes, and another which takes
place among the guests seated in darkness. Darkness and light continue
throughout the book until the play ends with "lights on."

The People Could Fly: American Black Folktales
Virginia Hamilton. Illustrated by Leo and Diane Dillon. Knopf,
ISBN 0-394-86925-7. $12.95. Read aloud.   *Ages 6–up.*

In the retelling of twenty-four tales, traditional and personal, Virginia
Hamilton divides her selections into animal tales, tall tales, supernatural
tales, and "slave tales of freedom." The material grows in power and im-

pact, and the title story finishes the book with a sweep of imagery and movement. Her notes, following the stories, discuss their oral origins and discuss their impact on a slave population. The Dillons' illustrations are gray, black, and white vignettes that echo the mood of the text.

A Wave in Her Pocket: Stories from Trinidad

Lynn Joseph. Illustrated by Brian Pinkney. Clarion,
ISBN 0-395-54432-7. $13.95. ***Ages 8–12.***

Fortunate children in Trinidad have a "tantie," a grandaunt who tells stories. Lynn Joseph, one of the lucky ones, has collected her tantie's chilling, tantalizing best into a unique whole. Many of the tales are rooted in the countries of West Africa and all are superb for reading aloud.

Tantie's stories begin on a family outing to the beach. Lynn and her cousins not only *hear* about a soucoyant (a person who changes into a bloodsucking ball of flame at night), but also *see* one. As each story is told, it will be understood on different levels, and a cumulative depiction of a clever, appealing old woman emerges.

Puss in Boots

Charles Perrault. Illustrated by Fred Marcellino. Farrar, Straus and Giroux,
ISBN 0-374-36160-6. $14.95. ***Ages 5–9.***

On the jacket looms Puss's furry face under a jaunty musketeer's hat in the style of classical heroic portraits. After that, throughout the book, Puss assumes a more modest scale in his traditional role of tiny operative behind monumental events. Through guile and subterfuge, he makes contacts in high places and wins the day for his less resourceful human master.

Fred Marcellino's pictures, which borrow from many seventeenth-century sources, are dramatic, witty, and intelligent with detail.

Rumpelstiltskin

Retold and illustrated by Paul O. Zelinsky. Dutton,
ISBN 0-525-44265-0. $13.95. ***Ages 5–9.***

According to folklore, a poor miller's lovely daughter must spin straw into gold or die. An odd little gnome-type man called Rumpelstiltskin agrees to perform the impossible task for her, but only when the young woman promises him her firstborn. The maid does that, then marries the king. They soon have a child and Rumpelstiltskin comes to collect.

Richly depicted in Paul Zelinsky's oil paintings of a medieval Flemish landscape and turreted castles filled with splendid period details, the old story never loses its hold.

Funny and Riveting

At approximately five to eight years old, most kids who are going to do it, cast their lot with the committed readers of the world. For youngsters who are struggling, funny books and I-Can't-Put-It-Down books will give a shove in the right direction.

Hey Willy, See the Pyramids
Maira Kalman. Viking/Kestrel,
ISBN 0-670-82163-2. $14.95.   *Ages 5–8.*

A big sister named Lulu tells ten very short stories, some about cross-eyed dogs dining at fancy-schmancy restaurants, one about Maishel Shmelkin, who forgot his pants, and one about Cousin Ervin, who has a green face and orange hair. All are illustrated in lots of primary colors and 1950s kitchen-counter-linoleum patterning. Yes, the art quotes from other artwork; yes, it's another try at postmodernism for children and with the requisite amount of ironic detachment to make it qualify. But this book has genuine warmth. A party for endearing oddballs takes place in the sunshine. Attending are many relatives, many twins, many animals, and so many sweet mutants you may feel off balance but you won't feel bored.

John Patrick Norman McHennessey—The Boy Who Was Always Late
John Burningham. Crown,
ISBN 0-517-568055. $12.95.   *Ages 4–8.*

John Patrick is a child who is always late to school, and for very good reasons: a crocodile tries to eat his book bag, a lion chases him up a tree, a tidal wave carries him off. The adventures are spelled out in full bright colors, while his attempts to convince his teacher (drawn as an enormously predatory figure) are in somber tones. The illustrations are mixed media. Childlike handwriting decorates the endpapers where the humor begins and never misses a beat.

Julius, the Baby of the World
Kevin Henkes. Greenwillow,
ISBN 0-688-08943-7. $12.95.   *Ages 4–up.*

When Lily found out she was going to be a big sister she was the best big sister in the world. She sang lullabies to the unborn baby, she gave him things, she told him secrets. But—"After Julius was born, it was a different story.

"Trust me. Babies are dreadful," a new Lily says candidly, and while child and adult reader laugh aloud Kevin Henkes works his text and pictures to a more than reasonably happy conclusion.

I Hate English

Ellen Levine. Illustrated by Steve Bjorkman. Scholastic,
ISBN 0-590-42305-3. $13.95.   *Ages 5–8.*

Although she was an excellent student at her old school in China, Mei Mei resists learning English at her new school in New York. She quickly learns to comprehend what her teacher is saying, but refuses to speak or write a language she considers strange and ugly. She steadfastly, and understandably, maintains, "I hate English!" Humorous, sketchy watercolors enhance this story of the assimilation of a reluctant little immigrant. It will appeal especially to children learning to cope with a new language—or with new classmates.

Tar Beach

Faith Ringgold. Crown,
ISBN 0-517-58030-6. $14.95.   *Ages 5–8.*

Tar Beach is the roof of a Harlem apartment building where Cassie Louise Lightfoot spends hot summer evenings with her family. She lies there under the heavens, feeling rich. To own anything, she knows, all she need do is fly up over it and it becomes hers.

In bold and energetic brushstrokes, bright lights and stars sparkle against dark sky. In an affecting, autobiographical book a little girl uses her imagination to free herself as the slaves did—by "flying" away.

Aunt Flossie's Hats (& Crab Cakes Later)

Elizabeth Fitzgerald Howard. Illustrated by James Ransome. Clarion,
ISBN 0-395-54682-6. $14.95.   *Ages 3–6.*

Sunday afternoons are special times for Aunt Flossie's two visiting nieces. Her house is as comfortable and reassuring as Flossie herself; it's "full of stuff and things"—and those hats! Each has a story worth telling. The dark blue one with red feathers reminds Aunt Flossie of the parade at the end of the Great War. One hat smells of smoke from the Big Fire in Baltimore.

The book's illustrations, while representational, are refreshingly paint-erly. Brushstrokes and daubs of rich color skillfully shape people (here an African-American family), objects, textures, and a believable place. Ran-some's work makes us feel this family's pleasure in just being together.

Uncle Wizzmo's New Used Car
Rodney A. Greenblat. Harper and Row,
ISBN 0-06-022097-X. $13.95.   *Ages 4–8.*

Two kids go with their uncle to buy a used car. Their outing with Uncle Wizzmo takes them past lurid signs, strip malls, motels, and fast-food joints which are not just blots on the landscape—they *are* the landscape. Greenblat's art includes all this clutter and crummy taste in a matter-of-fact way. His acceptance—the same as a child's—makes the pictures and book a delight. Turnpike Larry's used-car lot is a surrealistic wonderland; driving into it is like going down the rabbit hole. One car looks like a bowl of fruit, another like a bunny. But Uncle Wizzmo makes a deal on a rela-tively normal-looking car that wears a great big smile on its grille, and he and the kids drive happily home.

If You Give a Moose a Muffin
Laura Joffe Numeroff. Illustrated by Felicia Bond. HarperCollins,
ISBN 0-06-024405-4. $12.95.   *Ages 4–8.*

The proverbial warning against letting a camel's nose in the tent appar-ently applies to a moose as well; in this instance, one of the hulking creatures lumbers into the house to obtain homemade blackberry jam. The jam will go with the muffin that a boy has rashly given him. (This is the very lad who, in an earlier book, was unwise enough to "give a mouse a cookie.") Augmented by cheerfully ridiculous illustrations, and with a rhythmic, circular text, this book brims with chaos and infectious nonsense.

The Adventures of Isabel
Ogden Nash. Illustrated by James Marshall. Joy Street/Little, Brown,
ISBN 0-316-59874-7. $14.95.   *Ages 4–8.*

Intrepid Isabel is the feisty little brain child of versifier Ogden Nash. Here illustrator James Marshall makes her even funnier and more sly than she was at her original conception some forty years ago. With her big bow ribbon, spectacles, and serious handbag she is, on first glance, simply an earnest little party. However, a second look and the reader's natural suspi-cion sets in—is this sweet young thing the coldblooded killer kid who eats a live bear, turns a witch to milk (which she promptly drinks), and changes a doctor with a poised medicine-filled syringe to jelly? Isabel does this, all of it, by simply looking directly into the eye of the animal or person and saying "BOO TO YOU." A funny girl, this one has fish blood. Marshall's superb book includes two kinds of humor that rarely rub shoulders—raucous and deadpan.

Some beginning reading books, **Amelia Bedelia** (Morrow), the **Henry and Mudge series** (Bradbury), **George and Martha** (Houghton Mifflin), **The Stupids series** (Houghton Mifflin), **The Golly Sisters** (Harper-Trophy), and Crosby Bonsall's **The Case of the Hungry Stranger** (HarperCollins) are as satisfying reads as anyone will experience in life. They help slide youngsters triumphantly and happily into the world of the literate.

For children with a scientific bent several elementary science series will do the same. Consider the **Step into Science series** (Random House) or the **Let's Read and Find Out series** (HarperCollins).

On occasion, timely nonfiction shocks adults as much as it teaches children. **The House That Crack Built** by Clark Taylor (Chronicle) uses the old rhyme "The House That Jack Built" to show, in a handsome heart-breaking picturebook, where and why crack-cocaine starts, how it travels, and what it does.

More comfortably acceptable is the different but equally remarkable **Eyewitness Junior series** from Alfred A. Knopf.

Eyewitness Junior: Amazing Mammals; Amazing Spiders
Alexandra Parsons. Photographs by Jerry Young. Knopf,
ISBN 0-679-80224-X; 0-679-80226-6. $6.95 each. **Ages 7–9.**

What does the camel *really* keep in its hump? Which animal can hear a worm wriggling in a field? Which spider makes a good house pet? Why don't spiders get caught in their own webs? Children can find answers in this lively series. Both books offer a real-life look at amazing but true animal behavior. Each is chock-full of fascinating facts, with photos so lifelike you can almost feel a tiger's fur or the hair on a spider's back. The *Eyewitness Junior* series includes other titles, among them are *Birds; Snakes; Cats; Poisonous Animals; Frogs and Toads; Lizards; Crocodiles and Reptiles; Cars; Flying Machines; Animal Disguises; Armored Animals; Bats; Beetles; Tropical Birds.*

The Ladybug & Other Insects
Weather
Fruit
Colors
Pascale De Bourgoing. Scholastic,
ISBN 0-590-45235-5; 0-590-45234-7; 0-590-45233-9, 0-590-45236-3.
$10.95 each.   ***Ages 5–8.***

Four sturdy, appealing, spiral-bound books are just the right size for little hands. Each gives a fascinating overview of the title topic, and each contains a number of see-through plastic pages that change the pictures. For example, on one page a ladybug lays her sticky eggs on an aphid-covered leaf. Flip the transparency to see what happens to the eggs. Turn transparent pages in other books and see a sunny scene turn rainy, or a trio of fruits show their insides. Children will look, read, learn, and heartily enjoy.

Predator!
Bruce Brooks. Farrar, Straus and Giroux,
ISBN 0-374-36111-8. $13.95.   ***Ages 7–10.***

Excepting man, all animals must spend the major part of their time hunting food while others hunt for them. From pitcher plants to whales to ant lion larva to electric eels, the preying and the preyed upon are examined in this short (seventy-two-page) well-written volume about managing to stay alive. Full-color elegant photographs further clarify a text that is pristine and precise in its descriptions.

The Magic School Bus Lost in the Solar System
Joanna Cole. Illustrated by Bruce Degen. Scholastic,
ISBN 0-590-41428-3. $13.95.   ***Ages 7–10.***

Ms. Frizzle's class is disappointed when the planetarium they want to see is closed. However, on the way back to school, an amazing thing happens. The Magic School Bus tilts back, blasts off, and zooms through space. It visits all the planets and the students see and learn a lot, but will anyone believe it really happened? Like a string of cartoons with additional text, this heavily illustrated book will lure most young readers and teach them about the solar system. Other titles in this series are: . . . *At the Waterworks;* . . . *Inside the Human Body;* . . . *Inside the Earth;* . . . *On the Ocean Floor.*

Children whose families or friends read in Spanish as well as in English will particularly enjoy:

Song of the Chirimia/La Musica de la Chirimia

Jane Anne Volkmer. Translated by Lori Ann Schatschneider. Carolrhoda, ISBN 0-87614-423-7. $12.95. **Ages 5–9.**

This Guatemalan folktale recounts the legend of the chirimia, the musical pipe whose song is even sweeter than the sound of the birds. When young Black Feather asks Moonlight to marry him, she agrees, but only if he can learn to sing like the birds. Black Feather tries. He tries very hard, and finally he is helped by the Great Spirit of the Woods. Vibrant illustrations, based on ancient Mayan stone carvings, decorate the book.

Family Pictures/Cuadros de Familia

Carmen Lomas Garza. Children's Book Press, ISBN 0-89239-050-6. $12.95. **Ages 6–12.**

In the Hispanic community of Kingsville, Texas, lives a young girl, who narrates the story of her own family and its traditions. She includes her dream of becoming an artist, so the reader, seeing the illustrations, understands the girl does indeed fulfill her ambition.

Uncle Nacho's Hat/El Sombrero del Tío Nacho

Adapted by Harriet Rohmer. Illustrated by Veg Reisberg. Spanish version: Dr. Alma Flor Ada, Rosalma Zubizarreta. Children's Book Press, ISBN 0-89239-043-3. $13.95. **Ages 4–8.**

His niece Ambrosia brings Uncle Nacho a brand-new hat because the old one is full of holes. Whenever he tries to get rid of the ancient sombrero it somehow gets back to him. One way or another Uncle Nacho's hat comes home. The amusing story, in Spanish as well as in English, is complemented by the bold and bright-as-shellacked-paint illustrations typical of most books from the Children's Book Press.

Each of the previous books may, probably will, lead children to others, perhaps by the same author or on similar subjects. But there are other books no child should reach age eight without having a chance at.

Among them are **Anno's Italy** and **Anno's Math Games** by Mitsumasa Anno; the **Babar** books by Jean or Laurent de Brunhoff; **Brother**

Eagle, Sister Sky by Susan Jeffers; *A Chair for My Mother* by Vera Williams; *Charlotte's Web* by E. B. White; *Chicka Chicka Boom Boom* by Bill Martin, Jr., and John Archambault; *A Day with Wilbur Robinson* by William Joyce; *Eloise* by Kay Thompson; *The Emperor's New Clothes* by Hans Christian Andersen; *The Garden of Abdul Gasazi* by Chris van Allsburg; *Goggles!* by Ezra Jack Keats; *Going Home* by Nicholasa Mohr; *Goodnight Moon* by Margaret Wise Brown; *Harriet the Spy* by Louise Fitzhugh; Trina Schart Hyman's *Hershel & the Hannukah Goblins* and her *Snow White*; Richard Egielski's and Arthur Yorinks's *Hey, Al* and *It Happened in Pinsk*; *Honey, I Love* by Eloise Greenfield; *The Hundred-Penny Box* by Sharon Bell Mathis; *Jerusalem, Shining Still* by Karla Kuśkin; *Just-So Stories* by Rudyard Kipling; **The Little House series** by Laura Ingalls Wilder; *Madeline* by Ludwig Bemelmans; *Make Way for Ducklings* by Robert McCloskey; James Marshall's **Miss Nelson series**; *Owl Moon* by Jane Yolen; *The Polar Express* by Chris van Allsburg; *The Porcelain Man* by Marcia Sewall and Richard Kennedy; *Ramona Quimby, Age Eight* by Beverly Cleary; Stephen Gammell's and Cynthia Rylant's *The Relatives Came*; *The Secret Garden* by Frances Hodgson Burnett; *Simon's Book* by Henrik Drescher; *The Story of Ferdinand* by Munroe Leaf; *Sylvester & the Magic Pebble* by William Steig; *The Three Robbers* by Tomi Ungerer; *Turtle Knows Your Name* by Ashley Bryan; *Where the Wild Things Are* and *Dear Mili* by Maurice Sendak; *Why Don't You Get a Horse, Sam Adams?* by Jean Fritz; *Why Mosquitoes Buzz in People's Ears*, illustrated by Leo and Diane Dillon; *Winnie-the-Pooh* by A. A. Milne; and your own family's choices as well as your own family's stories.

For Children Ages Eight and Up

Sideways Stories from Wayside School
Wayside School Is Falling Down
Louis Sachar. Illustrated by Julie Brinckloe; Joel Schick. Avon Camelot, ISBN 0-380-69871-4; 0-380-75484-3. $3.50; $2.95.   *Ages 8–12.*

Wacky Wayside School is unique. Built sideways, with thirty rooms piled atop each other, it lacks a nineteenth story because the builder forgot it. It provides a perfect setting for a long litany of nutty disasters. In the first book, Sharri falls asleep and rolls out the window; Joe counts all wrong and gets the right answers; Calvin is sent to deliver a note to the missing nineteenth floor. Kids will get hooked on the broad humor and twisted logic of these loosely connected stories. Who could resist the teacher in the second book who throws the computer out the window to demonstrate gravity? And who will be surprised that Wayside School's fire drill is announced by a cowbell? When it sounds, the school promptly fills with cows.

Dakota of the White Flats
Philip Ridley. Knopf,
ISBN 0-679-81168-0. $12.95.   *Ages 7–10.*

Ten-year-old Dakota is a girl who always has an idea. And the idea usually involves the heavy-duty assistance of her occasionally reluctant but always generous friend, Penelope—or Treacle—Duck. The two girls are somewhat rounded characters in a brilliant comic novel set in White Flats, a blue-collar section of London. That is home to a collection of fabulous nutballs, vividly portrayed.

Imaginative, well written, and witty, the book also has subtlety and some solid, savvy values. It's exactly the sort of reading that kids, and everyone who espouses children's literacy, will probably want to pass on to others.

The Mouse Rap
Walter Dean Myers. Harper and Row,
ISBN 0-06-02343-0. $12.95.   *Ages 8–11.*

Mouse is a handsome fourteen-year-old with a fondness for rapping, for his mom—he calls her his "mother person"—and for playing basketball. He is not fond of entering dance contests with his friend Sheri, or of robbing banks, or of his father, who has suddenly reappeared. However, when a televised treasure-hunter talks about an old bank robbery in which the loot was never recovered, Sheri's grandfather gets interested. Both he and another old man once worked for the robbers' leader. Soon Mouse finds himself embroiled in dance contests, pseudo–bank robberies, and an odd gang of old men and Harlem teenagers.

This funny novel is filled with the rhythm and rhymes of a talented rapper. Mouse springs forth as a fully realized, bona fide young man.

Matilda
Roald Dahl. Illustrated by Quentin Blake. Viking,
ISBN 0-14034-294-X. $4.50.   *Ages 9–up.*

Matilda is a genius at getting even with her crooked, cruel parents. Peroxide appears in her dad's hair tonic, superglue in his hat. But at school Matilda must match wits with the venomous Miss Trunchbull. What happens when something more than brainpower is needed? The answer lies in an array of funny characters, far-out happenings, and ingenious plots.

Oren Bell

Barbara Hood Burgess. Delacorte,
ISBN 0-385-30325-4. $15.   *Ages 9–11.*

Oren Bell, his tough and bossy twin, Latonya, and their brilliant little sister Brenda live in a haunted house in the middle of Detroit. As if the ghosts weren't enough, life in the 'hood is pretty scary. Terrible things are going on in the house next door, too. And Oren can't keep his grandaddy or his very best friend, Fred, out of it. Then, just as seventh grade is getting interesting with the new teacher's history project that might exorcise the Bells' ghost, the kids learn their school is scheduled for demolition. In a warm, loving, and impossible-to-put-down story, an impoverished African-American family displays two timeless survival skills—humor and courage.

Strider

Beverly Cleary. Illustrated by Paul O. Zelinsky. Morrow,
ISBN 0-688-09901-7. $14.95.   *Ages 9–12.*

Leigh Botts lives with his newly divorced mom in a ramshackle rented cottage in Pacific Grove, California. If Leigh sees a trucking accident on the TV news, he holds his breath until he's sure the trucker isn't his dad. One day on the beach, he comes across an abandoned dog with a certain look on its face. He muses, "I know what it feels like to be left behind, so I probably have that same look. . . ." At that moment Leigh's relationship with the canine he calls Strider begins. It comes to mean more to him than he ever expected, or wanted.

Baseball in April and Other Stories

Gary Soto. Harcourt Brace Jovanovich,
ISBN 0-15-205720-X. $14.95.   *Ages 12–up.*

Brief and poignant, each of the eleven stories features young Mexican-Americans struggling to grow up with few resources in an alien, materialistic society. Although Soto's characters—immigrants' children—share in the needs and desires of all young people, their parents' longings are in keeping with their own culture.

The title story, *Baseball in April,* highlights two brothers who make an unsuccessful bid for Little League status. While Michael turns to a girl for solace, the younger, Jessie, continues playing on a pickup team that, like much in their lives, simply dwindles away. Their endurance is, with unique sensitivity, made clear.

Shaka, King of the Zulus
Diane Stanley and Peter Vennema. Illustrated by Diane Stanley. Morrow,
ISBN 0-688-07342-5. $13.95
                                                                Ages 7–12.

In olive hues reflective of the often parched land of the Zulus, this pictorial biography relates the life of an obscure boy who grew to be one of the world's mightiest warriors and to forge a nation. Because of a small failure of the child's courage, young Shaka and his mother were cast out of his royal father's tribe. The boy never forgot his pariah status, and in the military fashion of the day, proved his courage to his own satisfaction. Without glossing over the ferocity of his nineteenth-century reign, the tone of Shaka's biography is restrained, yet proud. The illustrations—detailed, exact—repeat Zulu bead design and artifacts in the rhythm of an epic.

The Wright Brothers: How They Invented the Airplane
Russell Freedman. Photographs by Wilbur and Orville Wright.
Holiday House, ISBN 0-8234-0875-2. $16.95.
                                                                Ages 9–up.

Excellent mechanics by profession and inclination, the Wright brothers were also amateur photographers who left a detailed pictorial record of their work. Russell Freedman has written a lucid, exciting photo-biography using the brothers' own pictures.

The story opens on September 20, 1904, when Wilbur first flew an airplane in a complete circle and brought it back to its starting point. Here the author digresses to explain Wilbur and Orville's early fascination with bicycle mechanics as well as the intellectual leaps they made while inventing. The cumulative excitement will have readers on the edge of their seats, waiting for the moment when the brothers get their flying machine with its wires, rods, and braces into the air.

Rosa Parks: My Story
Rosa Parks with Jim Haskins. Dial,
ISBN 0-8037-0673-1. $17.
                                                                Ages 10–up.

On December 1, 1965, in the segregated American city of Montgomery,

Alabama, a woman named Rosa Parks refused to vacate her bus seat for a white man. This act incited an inevitable legal injunction against segregation on public transport. It also initiated a national civil rights movement. Haskins's book is about Parks's life, not just about one act of disgust. And it's as fully informative as it is fascinating.

Lyddie
Katherine Paterson. Lodestar,
ISBN 0-525-67338-5. $14.95.   **Ages 10–up.**

For thirteen-year-old Lyddie and her siblings, the bear who breaks into the family's Vermont cabin in 1843 seems to be a source of hilarity. Unfortunately, the animal really proves to be the first in a series of disasters that ultimately deprive Lyddie of her family and farm. The bear comes to symbolize all she endures, from her discovery of a runaway slave to her own virtual slavery in a tavern kitchen and later in a Lowell, Massachusetts, cotton mill. In a historical period when working conditions, especially for women, were extremely harsh, Lyddie copes by working even harder. Katherine Paterson shows a young woman of passion and fiber within the context of a well-told story.

Wolf
Gillian Cross. Holiday House,
ISBN 0-8234-0870-1. $13.95.   **Ages 10–up.**

Never knowing her father but living with his reliable mother, her grandmother, thirteen-year-old Cassie is accustomed to being sent on mysteriously sudden trips to stay with her mother. One night, after hearing puzzling noises at her grandmother's, Cassie is abruptly sent away. She finally finds mom living in an abandoned house with her boyfriend, an itinerant drama teacher, Lyall, and his teenage son. Cassie soon becomes embroiled in Lyall's latest teaching scheme—a day-long production featuring wolves. She also, most oddly, finds a package of yellow plasticine in her suitcase.

   Cassie's dreams and waking hours are filled with increasing menace—she sees images of a wolf and, more and more, senses threats of men and bombs. Gradually, she realizes that her father is an IRA terrorist and the plasticine is intended for explosives. An intelligent, powerful, psychological thriller.

Weetzie Bat
Francesca Lia Block. Harper/Charlotte Zolotow Book,
ISBN 0-06-447068-7. $3.50.   **Ages 12–up.**

In a town called L. A. lived Weetzie Bat, a high school girl with a bleached-white flattop, pink Harlequin sunglasses, sugar-frosted eye shadow, and a best friend named Dirk. When Dirk tells Weetzie he is gay, she hugs him and says, "Now we can duck hunt together." Life as they live it is almost perfect, except Weetzie Bat has three wishes. As in traditional fairy tales, the folkloric themes in this modern one are bona fide. The language, however, is a Southern California import. Perhaps the mores are too. Weird as the characters may seem to the rest of the country, the book's tone is sweet. Its mood and message are the same: love (with or without sensuality) includes everybody. *Parents may want to discuss this book with their children. They may also want to share these sequels to* **Weetzie Bat**, **Witch Baby**, *and* **Cherokee Bat**.

The Brave
Robert Lipsyte. HarperCollins/Charlotte Zolotow Book,
ISBN 0-06-023915-8. $14.95.   *Ages 12–up.*

Sonny Bear is seventeen and a heavyweight boxer who finds his own anger terrifying. Only half Moscondagas Indian, Sonny has never been sure he really belongs on the Res. In spite of Uncle Jake's generous wisdom, he runs away to New York. There he is plunged into unsavory company and a frightening drug scene. A New York Police Department member and former Harlem boxer offers the prickly young man help. Is it real? Whom and what can he trust? Written with strength and economy, the storyline moves like fists hammering at a punching bag as it portrays a confused boy's inner journey toward manhood.

Beyond these contemporary zingers, there are books that you may want to introduce to your children by the time they're twelve, because these are some of the great cornerstones in our literary life. Among them are **Alice in Wonderland** by Lewis Carroll; **Anne Frank: The Diary of a Young Girl**; **Bridge to Terabithia** by Katherine Paterson; **Canyons** and **Dogsong** by Gary Paulsen; **Child of the Owl** and **Tongues of Jade** by Lawrence Yep; **The Chronicles of Narnia** by C. S. Lewis; **The Dark Is Rising** by Susan Cooper; **The D'Aulaire's Book of Greek Myths**; **The Earthsea Trilogy** by Ursula LeGuin; **Gideon Ahoy!** by William Mayne; **Heartsease** by Peter Dickinson; **Huckleberry Finn** by Mark Twain; **The Island on Bird Street** by Uri Orlev; **Journey Home** by Yoshiko Uchida; **The Light Princess** by George MacDonald; **M. C. Higgins the Great** by Virginia Hamilton; **Narrative of the Life of Frederick Douglass** by Frederick

Douglass; *The Prydain Chronicles* and *The Remarkable Journey of Prince Jen* by Lloyd Alexander; *The Railway Children* by E. Nesbit; *Roll of Thunder, Hear My Cry* by Mildred Taylor; *So Far from the Bamboo Grove* by Yoko Watkins; *Tales of Uncle Remus* and *Further Tales of Uncle Remus* by Julius Lester; *Upon the Head of the Goat* by Aranka Siegal; *The Way Things Work* by David McCauley; *Where the Lilies Bloom* by Vera Cleaver and Bill Cleaver; *Wind in the Willows* by Kenneth Grahame; *A Wrinkle in Time* by Madeleine L'Engle; and your family's stories.

Guidelines to Choosing Books for Children From Birth to Six Years Old

Everyone, including experts, agrees it is important to begin reading to little ones early. For newborns, any book a parent or other caretaker enjoys reading in singsong comforting tones is a good choice.

Beginning in the first few months—

- Choose books that have good-size illustrations on every page, books with very little text.

Toddlers will soon enjoy counting books, ABC books, and a simple story from beginning to end—

- Choose books that appeal to you. Ask yourself, Is this book attractive, interesting, fun, instructive? Would I want to read it again? If you do, chances are your child will too.
- Choose books that deal with the familiar—familiar situations and familiar things. Sleeping, walking, eating, cribs, toys, bottles or breasts, Cheerios, yogurt, etc.
- Almost all little ones like books with realistic pictures of other babies. (One thick-paged book called *Babies* is a long-time favorite. Another, *El Mundo del Bebe*, published by Dutton, is a new favorite.)

As you look at a book for a three- to six-year-old, ask yourself—

1. Does the language in this book have emotional appeal? That is, does it speak in rhythms and tones children comprehend? Does it provoke laughter, curiosity? Does it comfort?
2. Do the pictures have emotional appeal? Does the book engage the child's visual and auditory senses? Is it a pleasure to see and to hear read aloud?

3. Does the book promote self-esteem? For example: does it include my child's heritage or background? In cases of adoption, does it include the child's birth heritage as well as the adoptive parents' heritage?
4. Does the book promote understanding of others; that is, does it include others' backgrounds and customs?

- Some children, early on, are interested in anything that moves—cars, trucks, airplanes. Some are interested in animals: dogs, cats, cows, etc. Respect that interest. Build on it by offering good, quirky books on whatever subject excites your child.
- Go for books that have stood the test of time. Move toward books that begin introducing the world outside the home.

Share the pleasure of the book. Share the content and the story. Talk about the characters as if they were real. For example: "Why did Cinderella let her sisters bully her?" "How did Grandfather Anansi get all the stories? His way was funny. Was it fair?"

Above all—know your child, respect her or him, trust your own judgment, show enthusiasm, and *read aloud.*

3

Videos

SMALL-SCREEN FILMS that have become part of childhood's core curriculum grow in numbers. A few more and more solid programs are thoughtfully produced, reflecting a changing view of childhood. Directors gentle their way into tough subjects, approaching in a unified consistent manner broad questions busy parents and day-care moms or dads can only field hit or miss.

Fire, pestilence, death that comes close, strangers, and other nightmarish realities were once the province of folktellers and families. Side by side with their little ones all day, mothers especially, and sometimes fathers, could see to their youngsters' learning. But 7:30 A.M. dropoff at day-care or preschool and 5:30 P.M. pickup preclude exclusive mentorship of anyone's offspring.

Big Bird is as important as a long-distance grandma and Mr. Rogers is as close as grandpa. Very young children throughout the world share these worthy electronic teachers. The same technology that destroyed widespread literacy is, in part, helping us raise our children with care. ABC-TV's Peter Jennings arranges a national town meeting to talk with our kids about AIDS; a year before, he talked with them about the war in the Gulf. And, watching either show, one senses it's about more than P. R. We're in trouble and everyone knows it.

Business, from Cap Cities to Coors, IBM to NBC, Pizza Hut to CBS, pushes reading.

Beyond reading and computing, what do we need to teach our children and what ways do we have to do it? In his essay "The Fraying of America" Robert Hughes takes issue with school curriculums, writing: "The future . . . will rest with people who can think and act with informed grace across ethnic, cultural, linguistic lines. . . . In the world that is coming, if you can't navigate difference you've had it" (*Time* magazine, December 3, 1992).

In time, of course, schools will improve. Teachers will be better educated and honored. Buildings will be shipshape and the walk or ride to them will be safe. For now, enrichment happens best in community-sponsored events, in libraries, in museums, and at home.

Video is a rich source. Our kids are comfortable with its vividness, its pace, and its demands. Long a negligent nanny, the tube can now be a conduit to mom and dad's taste, and a test of their creative discipline or ability to negotiate.

The children of the motivated have a you-are-there visual history available for the borrowing from public libraries. Ken Burns's *Civil War* is one example. There are others that go hand-in-well-fitted-glove with learning. *The Wonderful Potato, Sounder, Molly's Pilgrim* are titles that reach into the collective unconscious of children whose ancestry lies respectively in Ireland, Africa, East European Jewry. Their tones range from rational to schmaltz. Mr. Wizard lays on some scientific facts, *3-2-1 Contact* and *Mathnet* others. Rabbit Ears's series, *We All Have Tales,* tries to highlight universal human truths, as do a number of fine old and new companies.

Here, on film or tape, is where children can see with their own eyes, hear with their own ears, different people from and in different places. Little kids can watch others living together in harmony and disharmony. Everyone, everywhere, younger and younger, may soon come to know each is simply trying to learn the rules in order to get the rewards. Each filmed character, real or fictional, has ties, duties, obligations, and pleasures.

Watching, thinking about, and discussing the following cinematic experiences is provocative or funny, absolutely respectable, and the diametric opposite of passive.

For the Youngest

Between twenty months and two years children are ready to begin understanding video. For the most part it will be the music and motion accompanied by color that attract. Recognizable people—moms, dads, babies—involved in familiar activities such as eating, singing, dressing, walking are always interesting. Sometimes gentle animation is woven into a film's texture. Jim Henson's *Peek-a-Boo* (currently out of print), originally part of the not so memorable Play-Along Video Series, is still stellar, and possibly unique. Its cast of babies, though not sufficiently multicultural, is brilliant. These starlets do what babies and toddlers do. They move about,

8

48fall, pick themselves and other things up, smile, cry, and laugh. The un-named director of photography has a high and dry sense of humor and drama. Some other gems for little children are:

BabySongs
More BabySongs
Hi-Tops. 30 min. each. $14.95 each. **Ages 2–4.**

The remarkably produced first tape has several visual approaches: one song, "Rub a Dub," is performed in part by a puppet in a shower cap, another is performed in full by a marionette; all segments are introduced by animation that's gentle in color and tone. The ongoing live-action shots of real toddlers are outstanding. Children of all colors participate, sing and dance, shout and whisper. One song, "The Day I Took My Diapers Off," is such a helpful and irresistible rite of passage it has become a teeny classic. *More BabySongs,* the second in the long series that follows, is imaginative, fresh, and equally remarkable. The others can become repetitive.

Stories to Remember: Baby's Nursery Rhymes
Lightyear Productions, Hi-Tops/Media Home Ent.
25 min. $14.98. **Ages 15 mo–4 yrs.**

Sung by Phylicia Rashad to the sound of Jason Miles, this music video for very little children is a gentle, humorous one. It's adapted from *The Baby's Lap Book* by Kay Chorao; her illustrations, animated, remain tender and take on an additional stylishness. Dr. Foster goes to Gloucester in a time-honored but very funny fashion; Pussy Cat visits the Queen in London; Mary, Mary Quite Contrary has a new look. Little Bo-Peep's sheep are sweetly sassy, their mistress a bit of a kvetch. The Cat and the Fiddle sparkle. All retain traditional appeal.

Nonsense and Lullabyes: Nursery Rhymes
Michael Sporn/FHE. 27 mins. $9.98. **Ages 2–5.**

Here Michael Sporn sensitively invigorates eighteen classic nursery rhymes in flashy little episodes with a 1990s tempo. "Wynken, Blynken and Nod"; "The Crooked Man"; "Solomon Grundy" are among the traditional verses presented. The production brings irresistibly subtle, and not so subtle, new humor to customary acclaimed Anglo-Saxon nonsense.

The Video Music Box Story Songs
Random House Home Video. Approx. 30 min. $14.95. **Ages 2–4.**

Don Cooper sings stories and illustrates them with moving pictures that fit the text and mood of six tales. The first is about Fuzzy Caterpillar, who emerges from a real-life cocoon to munch his way through leaves and flowers. The children watching are as different from one another as the caterpillars in the garden are, and of almost as many colors. Like the emerging butterflies and the photography, they are wonderful to look at. Roger, in song two, is an endearing robot who, never mentioning that he's leading an exercise class, gets the children surrounding him, and viewers too, up and moving faster and faster in an aesthetically and physiologically satisfying dance game. Musically reminiscent of the well-paced work of Hap Palmer, the Video Music Box Man's work here is equally ingenious.

Raffi's Young Children's Concert
Raffi in Concert with the Rise and Shine Band
A & M Video. 50 min. each. $19.98 each.   *Ages 2–5.*

Raffi is the gentle guitarist-singer children open to as naturally as morning-glories to the sun. Even though the second tape (. . . *in Concert*) had a robust prepublication commercial success, turning "platinum" soon after announcement, Raffi still remains absolutely committed to his audience's well-being. A slightly eerie chap, he's a Mr. Rogers–type master musician, a giant talent in the field. On both tapes, his messages keep young eyes on the sky; his music keeps young limbs moving and spirits stirred.

Sharon, Lois and Bram series
A & M Video. Approx. 30 min. each. $14.98 each.   *Ages 3–6.*

These homey Canadian folksingers are the originators of Canadian Broadcasting's TV series "The Sharon, Lois and Bram Elephant Show," which won a Parents' Choice Award for Television in 1987. Now on home cassette, the smooth, polished group's top-form segments are cozy and comforting. Sharon, Lois and Bram's arrangements of "Eensy, Weensy Spider," "Pufferbellies," and "Little Rabbit Foo Foo" are musically unsophisticated yet affecting; their presentation is unstrained. Most noteworthy in the series are: *Sharon, Lois and Bram Sing A–Z* and *Sharon, Lois and Bram Live in Your Living Room.*

The Rory Story
Sony Kids' Video. 55 min. $14.98.   *Ages 2–5.*

Rory's well-loved hit melodies are much enriched by the addition of visuals. The singer herself is sweet and real as cane sugar. Her gang of characters, including the Incredible Piglets and Stinky Sox, are semiserious parodies of music-business people and they are fun. But avaricious Buster Chops is the malevolent persona of kid-vid, and he steals the show.

Sharon, Lois
and Bram

The Rory Story

Preschool Power
More Preschool Power
Preschool Power III
Concept Video. 30 min. each. $14.95 each.   *Ages 18 mo–4 yrs.*

Toddlers show their contemporaries how to tie their shoes, brush their teeth, comb their hair, button buttons, draw puppet faces on their own clenched fists, even build with "tools." Like all good teachers, these babies enjoy themselves and their subjects. Throughout, the sound of reggae, calypso, bebop, and rock keep actors and viewers smiling and moving. All three tapes have a core message that bears lots of repeating: knowledge is power and power is fun.

Ages Two to Four

By this time toddlers who know Dr. Seuss's books, as many over the world do, will welcome the most illustrious Seuss videos like old friends. The books should precede the videos. And for families that want to help develop high standards, the videos should be only the best of the series.

The Cat in the Hat Comes Back
Dr. Seuss's ABC
Hop on Pop
One Fish   Two Fish   Red Fish   Blue Fish
Random House Home Video. 30 min. each. $9.95 each.   *Ages 2–4.*

These versions of Dr. Seuss's books reflect and expand their humor. Children who know the storybooks see the familiar characters moving on screen, hear the concocted words and the upbeat comical music, and laugh aloud.

Each tape has several adaptations of Seuss Beginner Stories. Filmed in limited animation, all are handsome, and a few scenes are visually stunning. Use the "stop" button on your videotape player to frame any one of the aesthetically exciting pictures. Then get out the books and present little ones with a multimedia experience.

About this time, some solid information will come in handy. Hospital trips are possibilities for all kids and, for many, so are thoughts of fire.

Sesame Street Visits the Hospital
Sesame Street Visits the Firehouse
Random House Home Video. 30 min. each. $9.95 each.   **Ages 2–4.**

Television's greatest information and entertainment are, hands down, to be found on "Sesame Street." If Big Bird and the gang go along with children to the firehouse or to the hospital, sooner or later everything's going to be okay. Use as needed.

Consideration and courtesy for children as individuals are becoming important to the youngsters themselves. It's time for them, then, to begin learning that these attitudes are just as important from them. Puppeteer Shari Lewis helps with two enjoyable lessons: **Lamb Chop in the Land of No Manners** and **Don't Wake Your Mom.** Both are from A & M Video for children from three to six years old and cost $14.95 each. Equally practical though less smoothly produced is **Telephone Tips for Kids** (ages 2–5). It's twenty-one minutes long, about half the length of the two others, and costs $19.95. In addition to phone courtesy, it teaches phone safety for children home alone.

Learning to reach out knowledgeably to others is also the province of a tape aimed at friends of the deaf:

Sign-Me-a-Story
Random House Home Video. 30 min. CC. $14.95.   **Ages 3–6.**

While the hearing-impaired child is watching signed performances of up-to-date versions of "Little Red Riding Hood" and "Goldilocks and the Three Bears," the hearing child is also listening to Elaine Branko's cheery voice-over narration and learning the rudiments of sign language. In this version, live actors perform against picturebook backdrops. It's a jaunty production of two familiar stories that here promote self-esteem, inclusiveness, and, above all, communication.

Other witty and worthy cassettes for this age:

The Elephant's Child
Rabbit Ears/Random House. 30 min. $9.50.   **Ages 3–up.**

In an ordered avuncular tone that gives the film a hint of Kipling's tall-tale

Uncle Elephant

voice, Jack Nicholson tells the story of how the elephant got his nose. The elephant's child, insatiably curious, wants to know, "What does the alligator have for dinner?" The little pachyderm is socked, bopped, kicked, and picked on by elders who know it's an unmannerly (and dangerous) question. Superb drawings, only partially animated, suggest pictures in a book. The colors and the film's sounds seem filtered through a child's sight and hearing: elephants are a delicate fog gray, strange gentle calls hint at Africa, a broom whisks across a drum. There is a kick in wit and words as Elephant discovers that Alligator has anything she can catch for dinner—and that she even tries for little elephants' noses.

Count It Higher, Great Music Videos from Sesame Street
Sesame Street Home Video/Random House. 30 min. $9.95.   **Ages 3–6.**

In an irresistible MTV spoof, "SMV" (Sesame Music Video) Channel presents Count von Count as veejay for some impossible-not-to-remember-and-re-sing music videos. Audiences see and hear "Honk Around the Clock," "The Ten Commandments of Health" ("Wash your hands before you eat" is one), and "Letter B" (bewigged Beatle stand-ins sing to "Let It Be"). Children will learn, laugh, and enjoy. Parents will do the same.

Ella Jenkins/Live at the Smithsonian
Roundup Records. 28 min. $12.   **Ages 2–4.**

Ella Jenkins's showmanship, polished over years to a glowing patina, is restrained. She holds her audience of children at arm's length, no farther, no closer. Her presence is large; she's a woman of strong character. Her salt-and-pepper hair is close-cropped, and a vividly colored handcrafted African overblouse covers her from neck to waist. Everyone near her senses that, if need be, this woman could fold a little person to her ample self and comfort like nobody's business. But Ella's a proper sort, here to sing and teach. She does both as she involves children in movement, folk music, and wisdom. Whether she's written or adapted the program's tunes, each song is ten feet deep in tradition, horse sense, and morality. She makes unique musical experiences seem ordinary until, months after the video's first viewing, her face and songs slide back, homey as can be, into the viewer's dreams.

For Borrowing Only

As little ones are able to move comfortably and behave reasonably in public places, it's time to learn about the treasures the library holds. The following very expensive or very short videos are in many public library collections.

Waltzing Matilda
AIMS Media. 8 min. $49.95.   *Ages 2–5. (In libraries.)*

Waltzing Matilda is an eight-minute masterpiece. Animated clay animals perform the full story of the Australian folksong, depicting it on all its levels of humor, pathos, and bathos. Superb fun, the rousing tune, once heard, becomes instantly familiar. Photography by the South Australian Film Corporation imbues the production with authenticity that lightens eyes and hearts.

Truck Song
AIMS Media. 13 min. $49.95.   *Ages 4–8. (In libraries.)*

Truck Song will appeal to anyone from four and up who likes BIG trucks and simple travelogues. Based on the book by Diane Siebert, the real-life photography is excellent, and some of the road shots are exceptional. The narrative informs; the truck's narrow path in tough terrain thrills; and the pacing allows the viewer to digest the information and remain hungry for more.

The Dingles
Bullfrog Films. 8 min. $145.   ***Ages 4–7.*** *(In libraries.)*

Well-crafted, simple line animation expresses the eight-minute story's warmth. Doris Dingle, a cozy lady, has three cats "and she loved them with all her heart." Donna Dingle is a snotty Siamese; DeeDee Dingle spends her time tapping Doris Dingle's cheek; Dayoh Dingle, an all-round good guy, is digging his way to China. Suddenly a great thunderstorm comes crashing into their lives. DeeDee is flattened against the fence, and Donna and Dayoh and a flowerpot all get dumped into a rubble pile.

But the comfort of an after-the-storm hot bath is unsurpassed. There are warm milk and honey with butter on top for felines and a drop of catmint cordial for Doris. Narrator Emma Levine, reading from the book *The Dingles,* sounds as homey as Doris looks.

Stanley and the Dinosaurs
Churchill Films. 15 min. $325.   ***Ages 4–8.*** *(In libraries.)*

Readers of author Syd Hoff need no introduction to little Stanley, but this video will probably gain him additional fans. In an adaptation of Hoff's book, Stanley and his prehistoric pals are three-dimensional animated puppets who are threatened by dinosaur hordes. The other characters poke fun at Stanley's cerebral approach, until he proves conclusively that working smarter is far better than working harder. A rap narration, dancing cave dwellers, and singing dinosaurs provide pure pleasure for eyes and ears.

Morris Goes to School
Churchill Films. 14 min. $309.   ***Ages 4–8.*** *(In libraries.)*

Poor Morris the Moose! He can't read signs, he can't figure out money, and the kids make gentle fun of him. But Morris knows school can solve his problems, so he eagerly signs up. Being the only moose in a roomful of children is a little problem as Morris learns to read, to count, and to enjoy the predictable routines of a class for the very young. This adaptation of B. Wiseman's popular book features captivating clay-puppet animation, sweet humor, and a spectacular song.

Uncle Elephant
Churchill Media. 26 min. $365.   ***Ages 5–9.*** *(In libraries.)*

This three-dimensionally animated musical about Arnie, the little elephant whose parents disappear one evening while out sailing, is based on a book written and illustrated by the late humorist Arnold Lobel. When elderly Uncle Elephant learns Arnie's mom and dad are missing, he comes to take care of the boy. And what a taking-care it is. Beginning with a sing-along-song-filled train ride, moving on to teaching Arnie to play his trunk like a trombone and to laugh despite hard times, Uncle Elephant shows his nephew that "it's important to keep your trunk up." Which Arnie, despite some sad moments, manages to do. In a very happy ending his parents return and Uncle Elephant stays on as a loving counselor.

Available in stores as well as in libraries is a distinguished animated series some parents and grandparents may remember from the films and filmstrips of their own school days. We knew the studio then as Weston Woods. The home videos now are distributed under the Children's Circle label. More of these authentic, gracious-spirited films, all taken from children's books, have been made. None other is finer, of more remarkable charm, or more essential to the imaginative lives of preschool American children than—

Stories from the Black Tradition
CC Studios. 52 min. $14.95.   **Ages 4–8.**

Here, the first four of the five films-from-children's-books stem from African tales of mythic stature. These elegant animated stories include (1) the tale of the great trickster, Anansi, who holds all the world's stories, (2) the saga of Mufaro, whose kind and beautiful third daughter is a Cinderella of sorts, (3) Mosquitoe's reasons for buzzing people's ears, (4) the legend of the Village of Round and Square Houses, where men and women live separately. Each one is a treasure. They are followed by an American-African story, "Goggles!" written and illustrated by the late chronicler Ezra Jack Keats. The verbal, visual, and aural artistry of this collection makes it basic to every child's video library. For black children, what can one say? Such a heritage makes life fuller.

Next, though not necessarily in order of excellence, are:

Happy Birthday, Moon, and Other Stories for Young Children
CC Studios. 30 min. $14.95.   **Ages 3–7.**

Only the title film, about the bear who hears his echo and thinks it's the moon, won a CINE Golden Eagle. But the second film, "Peter's Chair" by

Ezra Jack Keats, is also distinguished. It tells of Peter's new baby sister, who seems to be taking over his house, his highchair, his mama and daddy. "Three Little Pigs" is the traditional tale told in traditional pictures by Eric Blegvad. However, a warning—in this version the third piggy dines on the vanquished wolf. No bloody parts, but every morsel is savored.

The other stories include two rhymes—the "Owl and the Pussycat," with paintings by Barbara Cooney, and "The Napping House," which is illustrated by Don Wood.

The Maurice Sendak Library
CC Studios. 35 min. $19.95.   *Ages 3–up.*

The triumphal procession of Maurice Sendak's books—"Nutshell Kids," "Where the Wild Things Are," and "In the Night Kitchen"—has in this animated production bearing, mien, and manner. Flat-headed and chubby, Sendak's characters move with inexplicable stature across the screen. They manage to be both funny and noble. The last segment consists of a meeting with the master himself. Many kids may not care about the interview with Sendak, but many, many parents will.

Owl Moon and Other Stories
CC Studios. 35 min. $19.95.   *Ages 4–8.*

Late one moonlit winter evening in New England, a girl is, for the first time, allowed to search with her father in the forest for the Great Horned Owl. It's a breathless, all-absorbing time the girl will not forget. She and her father are close in a way that will not happen again. Author Jane Yolen, narrating, uses a tone crystal as the night, but her telling of the tale is warm.

Other stories here include animated versions of Jack Kent's "The Caterpillar and the Polliwog," Mwenge Hadithi and Adrienne Kennaway's "Hot Hippo" and the long-loved "Time of Wonder," about summer on an island in Maine. Each story segment has its own individual color, tone, and pacing. The last three are small treasures; "Own Moon" is a great one.

The Amazing Bone and Other Stories
CC Studios. 40 min. $22.45.   *Ages 5–9.*

Although the tape's other stories ("John Brown," "Rose and the Midnight Cat," "A Picture Book for Harold's Room," "The Trip") are all based on prize-winning books, it's the title tale that's stellar. Pearl, a pretty young pig, is out strolling on a spring day when she meets a talking bone. The

Where the Wild Things Are

bone not only talks, but is even well spoken and well mannered. He's also courtly. He protects our Pearl from various villains, most notably from a dastardly fox in Saville Row duds. The minimalist animation, like William Steig's line drawings, is simple as a Shaker and quite as clean. With impeccable taste, John Lithgow narrates an impeccable manuscript.

Madeline's Rescue
CC Studios. 30 min.   *Ages 4–8. (In libraries.)*

Charming Madeline, the little girl who lives in a vine-covered house in Paris, invites a heroic dog, Genevieve, to join her and the eleven girls who are boarded and schooled at Miss Clavell's. Besides this tale, two other Bemelmans stories are included on a film that has aged well and is occasionally available on television.

The Snowman
CC Studios. 30 min. $14.95.   *Ages 3–6.*

An authentic "take" from the book by Raymond Briggs, this gentle tale is about a fair-haired boy. The boy builds a snowman. The snowman melts and we feel the boy's sadness in moving pictures that are painterly, delicate, and evocative.

The book each of these Children's Circle films is based on is easily available from the library or in paperback from many video outlets and bookstores. Encourage your child to enjoy books and films by providing both. The financial costs can be negligible, the literacy profits inestimable.

Ages Five to Eight

Uncommonly good videos also exist for kindergartners and primary grade children. Several come from Canadian TV.

The Tender Tale of Cinderella Penguin
Smarty Pants. 30 min. $14.98.   ***Ages 3–up.***

In the title segment handsome graphics and the hilarious surprise of seeing Cinderella as a penguin who loses her flipper, have style as well as a twist on tradition. In this adaptation, the Prince goes hunting for the foot that fits (webbed, of course). Canada's National Film Board produced this and the tape's other tales—the intriguing "Metaporphoses," the gallant "Mr. Frog Went a Courting," the fanciful "The Sky's Blue," and the multileveled Eskimo legend "The Owl and the Raven." They make up a lighthearted collection of witty films that aim high, strike the funny bone, and stimulate the imagination.

Peep and the Big Wide World
Smarty Pants. 30 min. $14.98.   ***Ages 3–up.***

Peter Ustinov narrates the story of Peep, a newly hatched chick who is bright, slightly bold, and absolutely endearing. With two feathered friends, Quack the difficult duck and Chirp the temperamental robin, Peep starts off on a journey. Each imaginative episode is amusing and stylish. Each achieves remarkable standards for multileveled animated entertainment.

Our country's folklore includes some tales that have been irresistibly transposed to film:

The Tender Tale of Cinderella Penguin

Pecos Bill

Sony Video/Rabbit Ears. 30 min. $14.95.   ***Ages 4–9.***

The hilarious American tall tale about Baby Bill who falls out of a wagon train headed west is read by Robin Williams. His tone *almost* defeats disbelief as the infant cheerfully adopts a coyote family, grows, rides a cyclone, grows some more, and comes to be known as Pecos Bill. Tim Raglin's line drawings and color illustrations are subtle, funny, and masterful. His drawing of the great Pecos Bill with rump exposed is as affectionate as williams's voice. as the story unfolds to Ry Cooder's music, we hear sagebrush sounds and see minimalist animation. The production, highspirited and rambunctious, amiably reminds us of what we used to think we were.

The Legend of Sleepy Hollow

Sony Video/Rabbit Ears. 30 min. $14.95.   ***Ages 7–10.***

The new schoolmaster has arrived in Old tarrytown. His name is Ichabod Crane, and he's as thin as his piety. Spying a wealthy farmer's daughter (Katrina), his heart and his greed leap up, but Katrina has her eye on hearty, handsome Brom bones. The legendary horseman enters; the plot thickens; earnest Ichabod is terrified. Washington Irving's very good story becomes—with Robert Van Nutt's illustrations, Tim Story's music, and

Glenn Close's narration—an elegant video production. The animation, especially in the square-dance scene, is superb.

Folk and fairy tales from many other lands exist on film.

Four Asian Folktales

Video Presentations. 48 min. 2 cassettes, $39.95. ***Ages 5–8.***

Children's librarian Rae Bass hosts these four folktale-based puppet plays produced at the Seattle Public Library. The first tape includes the Japanese "Aniraku," an Asian version of Rumpelstiltskin, and the "Kyogne Stories," two slyly hilarious plays. On the second cassette is the Chinese "Brocade Slipper," a Cinderella-type tale with a fish for a godmother; it is performed by hand and rod puppets. In "Uncle Toad and the Jade Emperor," a Vietnamese folktale, shadow puppets tell the story of a drought and the travelers who journey to plead for the emperor's help.

The Falcon

Children's Television Consortium. 60 min. $19.95. ***Ages 8–12.***

Filmmakers and actors from the United States and the Republic of Georgia worked together to produce the film version of a well-loved Eurasian folktale, *The Falcon*. Anna, a young woman with two tormenting sisters, receives a magical gift, the feather of a falcon. The feather becomes a prince whom Anna must rescue by crossing "nine mountains to the tenth kingdom." The tone, the costumes, the setting, and the idiomatic translation are excitingly genuine in this mesmerizing and funny film.

East of the Sun, West of the Moon
Anansi
Jack and the Beanstalk
The Monkey People

Rabbit Ears Productions. 30 min. each. $9.95 each. ***Ages 5–9.***

We All Have Tales Series (Rabbit Ears Productions), is a video series of the world's folktales. The stories center on "things . . . [children] see, think, and dream." Glenn Close, Jack Nicholson, Denzel Washington, Robin Williams, and others of like renown narrate. The film's writers, artists, and musicians also have a core of serious work to their credit. Some pieces fall

East of the Sun, West of the Moon; Jack and the Beanstalk

into film critic Charles Champlin's category of "brave, imperfect tries." Others—two, perhaps three, in this Rabbit Ears lineup—achieve stature.

East of the Sun, West of the Moon is a place where one courageous young woman must go to free her enchanted lover. Knowing it will be a treacherous journey, she sets out. Exquisite paintings and a moving, moody but well-controlled symphonic score add dignity to her epic journey. The story is based on Scandinavian folklore but its themes are integral to all human codes. *We strongly urge parents to view this with their children so families can discuss ideas and questions the film raises.*

African-American children will be particularly pleased by Rabbit Ears's spectacular version of *Anansi.* A brilliantly designed film with handsome graphics, it shows how the clever spider, Anansi, tricked Snake into giving him all the world's stories. The group UB40 provides the Jamaican sound, and Denzel Washington narrates with glee. Little boys, especially, respond pridefully to Anansi's maleness.

Jack and the Beanstalk is the familiar Anglo-Saxon story, here cleverly scored by the Eurythmics' Dave Stewart and wittily narrated by Monty Python's Michael Palin. Jack is not as dumb as he used to be and he's a good deal funnier. When the klutzy slim-witted giant begins, "Fe Fo Fi Fum I smell the blood of an Englishmun . . . ," children will shiver and giggle simultaneously. Here is a legend securely rooted in human frailties and strengths.

In *The Monkey People* Raul Julia narrates the fable of the Amazon rain forest people who grew lazier and lazier day after day after day. Artist Diana Bryan depicts them in handsome silhouette, which is minimally animated. It's one of the few in the Rabbit Ears *We All Have Tales* series that moves with humor in the quick time youngsters have come to expect of TV.

NOTE: *You may want to begin with the tape that is most clearly connected with your own background. All are steeped in universal human values; all are slow-paced.*

The Monkey People

The Red Shoes
Family Home Entertainment. 30 min. $14.95. **Ages 5–8.**

Ossie Davis narrates his version of Hans Christian Andersen's fairy tale. As Ossie tells it, the heroine is a downtown kid who moves uptown and leaves her very best friend behind and lonely. His moral, however, is much the same as the old Dane's.

Beauty and the Beast
Lightyear Productions, Hi-Tops/Media Home Ent.
27 min. $14.95. **Ages 6–10.**

This adaptation of the eighteenth-century fairy tale about the youngest of three daughters who takes her father's place as the Beast's captive, deals with love—unsentimentalized, strong. Mordicai Gerstein's animated paintings are thin-lined and airy; light seems to come from behind the watercolor washes, reflecting the story's themes of illusion and reality. Mia Farrow narrates comfortingly. Her tone and timing as she moves from one voice to the next remind the listener that it is, after all, make-believe. Although as different from that of Disney's remarkable, animated version as it is from that of Jean Cocteau's early-twentieth-century black-and-white film, Farrow's telling is as singular.

Among modern fairy tales and allegories for children, nothing in literature or film surpasses C. S. Lewis's *The Chronicles of Narnia.* The film series was lavishly and well produced by BBC under the following titles: *The Lion, the Witch and the Wardrobe, The Silver Chair,* and *Prince Caspian/Voyage of the Dawn Treader.*

The Lion, the Witch and the Wardrobe
Public Media Video. Approx. 169 min. 2 cassettes, $29.95.   *Ages 6–up.*

No child whose mother tongue (biological or adoptive) is English should reach the age of twelve without having a chance to read the book *and* see the WonderWorks version of C. S. Lewis's *Chronicles of Narnia.* In the early forties four young Brits, two sisters and two brothers, are scooted out of the London blitz to safety and, as they see it, to boredom in the English countryside. Their escape from ennui is through an old wardrobe (closet) into the fantastical land of Narnia, where good is Very Good, bad is a silvery witch, and Ultimate Good (God?) is a kingly lion named Aslan. Unless it is pointed out to them, children will probably neither know nor care much about the Christian allegory and symbolism. Narnia is a rattling fine yarn and in this screenplay the acting, writing, production, and direction are as rich as Croesus.

Video information on children in other cultures and on world problems exists. **Where in the World: Mexico** and **Where in the World: Alaska** from Children's International Network (28 min., $14.95 each), while somewhat thin, certainly suggest that people, actions, and things are perceived differently in different places. Just as well intended but far richer in information and entertainment values are three environmental issue tapes from Children's Television Workshop's program "3-2-1 Contact." **Down the Drain** (water), **The Rotten Truth** (garbage), and **You Can't Grow Home Again** (rain forests) star the well-spoken and mannerly Stephanie Yu, who takes viewers on trips through sewage plants and rain forests with equal verve and aplomb.

Spirit of the Eagle
Miramar Productions. 30 min. $19.95.   *Ages 6–up.*

Several unknown youngsters perform remarkably as inner-city kids on a wilderness field trip to bald-eagle country. The great bird, not long ago on the verge of extinction, once again rules the skies of the Pacific Northwest and Alaska. The kids phrase questions in authentic teen language and tone as the eagles hunt, mate, and raise their young. The footage leaves the viewer breathless.

There is round-the-world fiction that holds and informs young viewers.

Tommy Tricker and the Stamp Traveler
Family Home Entertainment. 101 min. $39.95.   **Ages 7–10.**

Tommy Tricker is a charming, shady smarty pants. His new friend Ralph, an endearing nerd, is a poor little rich boy who, like his dad, values collecting stamps. Nancy, Ralph's courageous sister, is clever, a girl with tact and a sense of fair play. When Tommy "sells" a stamp from their father's collection, an adventure begins for the trio of eight- to ten-year-old philatelists. This seventh production in the esteemed La Fête series from Canada involves traveling on a postage stamp to the other side of the world, moving in place and time—having fun in history and geography. These magical characters get hold of the heart; the plot sets it racing.

For youngsters who enjoy crafts and using their own hands, consider introducing origami, mime, or puppet-making as presented in **Look What I Made: Paper Playthings and Gifts** (Intervideo Association, 47 min., $14.95, ages 5–8), **Will You Be Mime?** (Krafty Kids, 35 min., $26.99, ages 5–8), **Make a New Friend** (Krafty Kids, Inc., 30 min., $29.95, ages 5–8).

And for the many families who move to new homes there is an acclaimed gem:

Let's Get a Move On!
Kidvidz. 25 min. $14.95.   **Ages 5–up.**

A support to any family moving from one home to another, this fine piece of work also points out, to new and old neighbors, how it feels to leave, and how it feels to arrive.

Juggletime
Jugglebug. 30 min. $19.95.   **Ages 5–up.**

"Step by step is how you learn to do it," says Professor Confidence (aka Juggler Dave Finnegan), who provides juggling-to-music so contagiously rhythmic that snails will step up their pace; boys and girls will burst out of their chairs and exert to learn. A funny, exuberant music video, this one teaches basic juggling pleasantly, with high-spirited patience.

Older Children

For Borrowing Only
Molly's Pilgrim
Phoenix/BFA Films and Video. 24 min. $325.   *Ages 6–10. (In libraries.)*

As she struggles to adapt to her new land, a young Russian immigrant transforms a traditional schoolroom Thanksgiving project into an enlightening lesson on religious freedom. This thoughtful, well-produced updating of Barbara Cohen's book lends renewed relevance to enduring American views.

The Tale of the Wonderful Potato
Phoenix/BFA Films and Video. 24 min. $300.   *Ages 8–14. (In libraries.)*

It's hard to imagine that anyone could make a fantastically fun story about the lowly potato, but this Danish import proves it can be done. Whimsical animation and a bevy of odd but fascinating little facts embellish the history of the lowly tuber, from its South American beginnings through its peripatetic global travels. Sometimes feared, sometimes reviled, ultimately valued for its adaptability and fecundity, the potato has changed the course of human history. This story will persuade kids to view their next bag of fries with the respect it deserves.

Koko's Kitten
Churchill Films. 16 min. $325.   *Ages 5–8. (In libraries.)*

A real-life documentary tells the story of Koko, the gorilla who learned to sign and made it known to her friend, the scientist, that she wanted a kitten. Her tender treatment of the pet, her sadness at its loss, and her eventual healing and willingness to accept another kitten will strike a chord with young viewers and with their parents. This is a touching story that conveys—far better than any lecture—a respect for life and feelings.

Harry and the Lady Next Door
Harry Comes Home
Barr Films. 20 min. each. $370–$420.   *Ages 5–9. (In libraries.)*

Not a herd of cows, a marching band, or any other distraction can dissuade the dog Harry's neighbor from singing high and loud. Only through the distraught pup's ingenious contribution to the soaring soprano's recital are peace and quiet restored. A talented canine actor shines in this marvelous melodic adaptation of Gene Zion's book. The same dog is the star of *Harry Comes Home,* which, while not quite as funny as the first film, is still captivating.

Mr. Marfil's Last Will and Testament
Phantom of the Bell Tower
Human Relations Media.
30 min. each. $175 each.   *Ages 10–up.* *(For school use.)*
Both of these are compelling detective games; each entices children to use math and to experience, that is, to *know,* the value of arithmetical skills. For school or other group use.

For school, library, or even home use there is nonfiction video that will help children intelligently move into and about their expanding lives.

The **You Can Choose series** has four titles: ***Dealing with Feelings, Being Responsible, Saying "No" to Smoking,*** and ***Cooperation*** (Elkind & Sweet/Live Wire Video). In each of these tapes aimed at six- to nine-year-olds the production is acceptable, the host equable, the subject essential.

The Drug Avengers
Lancit Media. 60 min. $36.95.   *Ages 5–9.*
Drug Avengers says it straight, "If you didn't get that pill from your mom and dad, you're going to end up feeling bad." Each of the five segments on the cassette is astonishingly creative, lively, and well produced. Cautionary messages have been woven with brilliance (the Brothers Grimm did it)— but with humor? It's a little miracle.

What Kids Want to Know About Sex and Growing Up (ages 8–12) produced by Children's Television Workshop, was first aired on TV and almost simultaneously was offered on home video for under $15. It is a straightforward and helpful piece of work that won rave reviews from critics and parents.

Growing Up in the Age of AIDS:
An ABC News Special Presentation
MPI Home Video/ABC News. 75 min. $24.   ***Ages 9–up.***

TV journalist Peter Jennings talks with young people about the AIDS scourge and what they must know about it. He handles the subject and the audience forthrightly, with respect.

Among the highest-quality live-action films from books are:

The Haunting of Barney Palmer
Public Media Video. 58 min. $29.95.   ***Ages 8–12.***

Chilling and eerie, as a ghost story should be, *The Haunting of Barney Palmer* is also assiduously multileveled. Barney, an imaginative nine-year-old boy, hears calls from an uncle who died before they could meet. Uncle Barnaby and some emotional skeletons in the family closet haunt the boy in what at first seems simply a tale of the supernatural. Scriptwriter Margaret Mahy is also the author of the novel the film's based on, so, not surprisingly, narrative and dialogue ring clear. Yvonne Mackay's direction of the child actors evokes some provocative performances in an altogether thrilling film.

Anne of Green Gables
Disney Home Video. 199 min. CC. 2 cassettes, $29.95.   ***Ages 8–up.***

Based on a 1908 novel about a twelve-year-old orphan sent to live on a farm with an elderly bachelor and his sister, this made-for-public-television movie is set on Prince Edward Island. The beauty of the location and the filming take hold of the heart from the first scene. The child, Anne, is bright, fanciful, curious, and hardly the laborer the old couple needs. Farmer Cuthbert finds her enchanting; his sister finds her trying. They are good people, accustomed to dealing with what life hands them. As they adjust to Anne, they change. It's an intelligent rite-of-passage film and it suggests that sometimes the most dramatic leaps are made by the old. While it holds youngsters spellbound, it may reignite wonder in their grandparents.

Sweet 15
Public Media Video. 110 min. $29.95.   ***Ages 8–10.***

Fourteen-year-old Marta Delacruz is looking forward to her *quinceañeras,* the traditional coming-of-age celebration that Mexican and Mexican-American girls have when they reach fifteen. Because Marta's father has a fine job, she is shocked to hear her parents say they have no money for her party. She behaves with understandable pique until she discovers the terrifying secret: her father is an illegal alien in imminent danger of discovery. For Marta it's painful to watch his inability to deal with the situation, his shame, and her mother's fear. While the man stands helpless, the girl acts. Her rite of passage is different from her anticipation of it, and far richer. The situation and culture portrayed are realistic, but the characterizations seem sentimentalized.

African Journey

African Journey
Public Media/WonderWorks. 174 min. 2 cassettes, $79.95.   ***Ages 10–up.***

On a visit to his father who is working in East Africa, Luke Novack, a high school student from Canada, meets a young man his own age, Themba Maposa. Luke comes on as a spoiled Westerner (the new ugly American?) but eventually learns manners and respect from the more mature Themba. Filmed in Zimbabwe, the moving pictures sweep the landscape. Occasionally they focus on real people going about their lives without affectation. Thin as the plot's structure is, and as a few of the characters remain throughout, the view of the boys' differing cultures is honest and affecting.

A Girl of the Limberlost
Public Media Video. 105 min. $29.95.   ***Ages 10–up.***

Set in the early 1900s in Indiana, this delicately directed film details a girl's struggle between her needs and her loyalties. Elnora Comstock has lived on a farm all her fourteen years. She loves the animals, insects, and plants of the Limberlost, the magnificent—and treacherous—acreage around her home. But now she wants a chance to go to high school. Kate, her widowed mother, barely hangs onto their farm; she believes life beyond the farm is a foolish dream for either of them. As Elnora meets other people, she becomes more troubled about her mother's unbending views. Then, watching, Elnora sees Kate does have laughter and love, but not for her. Soon both learn why. Each woman has been denied love, but by film's end both have grown. They can give love and accept it, though perhaps not fully to each other.

Some Not-to-Be-Missed Movies on Video Cassette

Robin Hood

Animated—see with family first:

Alice in Wonderland, Disney. Ages 4 up.
Robin Hood, Disney. Ages 3 up.
101 Dalmatians, Disney. Ages 3 up.
The Wind in the Willows, Disney. Ages 4 up.
Lady and the Tramp, Disney. Ages 4 up.
The Secret of NIMH, MGM/UA. Ages 4 up.

The Yellow Submarine, MGM/UA. Ages 5 up.
An American Tail, MCA Home Video. Not for children under 6.
Bambi, Disney. Not for children under 6.
Beauty and the Beast, Disney. Not for children under 6.

Live-Action—see with family first:

The Red Balloon, New Line Home Video. All ages.
The Black Stallion, CBS/Fox. Ages 6 up.
The Yearling, MGM/UA. Ages 6 up.
Sounder, Paramount. Ages 6 up; only with adult.
Vincent and Me, La Fête Productions. Ages 6 up.
E. T.: The Extraterrestrial, MCA. Ages 8 up.
The Journey of Natty Gann, Touchstone. Ages 6 up.
Empire of the Sun, Warner Bros. Ages 10 up; only with adult.
The Bear, RCA Columbia. Ages 8 up; only with adult.

Choosing Videos for Children

Read Reviews

Look for them in *Parents' Choice,* your newspaper, a local parenting paper, a parenting magazine. When you are in your public library, ask to see *Video Librarian, Booklist,* or *SightLines.* These publications offer information on recent releases soon to arrive in stores or libraries.

See Previews

Try tapes at the video store. As you view, ask yourself:

- Do the characters, music, plot, and photography come together to make a lively production?
- Does the theme promote the values I believe in?
- Does the content provoke thought?
- Does it encourage questions?
- Is the length suitable to my child's attention span?
- Is the film based on the kind of story I want my child to read?
- Is it a story that may appeal to people of different ages?

Ask Advice

Your children's librarian, your children's teacher, a video store manager who cares about kids, as well as other moms and dads you respect, are your local experts.

Remember, Good Videos

- Entertain and teach.
- Stimulate imagination.
- Lead a child to reading.

Initiating a Sensible Approach to TV and Home Video

1. Begin viewing with your child at about ten months. Start with shows that are slow-paced and have, overall, a gentle tone. Example: "Mr. Rogers' Neighborhood."
2. Avoid video that is overstimulating.
3. Select programs with segments that fit your child's attention span. Example: *Lamb Chop's Play Along*.
4. Limit viewing time. Start this habit early and remain consistent.

As Children Get Older

5. Make your family's choice of shows at the beginning of the week on a day-by-day basis. Build flexibility into your schedule to allow for program changes as well as for personal changes.
6. Make exceptions for special events—the annual national *Wizard of Oz* showing; a show with the stature of *Sarah, Plain and Tall*. These are television moments that can be highlights of family life.
7. Talk about television's two major offerings:
   - Entertainment
   - Information
8. Share your points of view on weighing entertainment values and informational values.

Remember, like adults, all kids need a chance to chill out. Entertainment or informational television can help as long as time and content are considered by parents and then negotiated fairly, with good humor.

NOW—About Commercials

Commercials offer a great opportunity to teach delaying gratification. A key phrase to use when your child wants a product being advertised is, "Let's put it on your birthday list." As the birthday approaches, take out the list. Ask your child to reconsider everything on it—and to number each item in order of current priority. Keep in mind: children grow from making choices; children gain from making choices on the basis of cost, need, appropriateness, and plain old "I want it."

Help children learn the difference between hype and fact. Help them learn the difference between fantasy and reality. Point out concrete examples.

- Discuss, for example, a cookie commercial and a public service announcement on eating veggies. Then let your child show *you* other examples.
- Make a chart for a favorite show. Head one column "Make Believe" and another "Real." Always praise correct answers.

Remember, by setting standards and limits for TV, and hanging onto them, you are giving your child an advantage no money can buy.

4

Audios

UNKNOWN TO MANY PEOPLE, the best music and verse for children have vigor. While the sound is simple, it is pristine. There is sentiment in it, but not sentimentality. It often demonstrates pure play and always shows solid, age-old instruction. The balladeer's voice sets the tone, not the synthesizer. Rhythm varies. It may contain pathos, but never bathos. The conciseness of the musical expression is in direct relation to its lasting appeal. There are no extraneous notes or words.

Women like Ella Jenkins, Diane Wolkstein, and Jackie Torrence have made this music and storytelling their life's work. Men like John Langstaff, Rafe Martin, and Jay O'Callahan do the same, working with preciseness and passion. Their stature is unquestioned, their vision clear, their standards picky. They communicate a sense that artistic excellence is exciting.

Their work, with that of others noted below, brings quality and style to youngsters of all classes. They sell nothing but sound and sense, whether heard on CDs with stereo or quadraphonic speaker systems or on rinky-dink car cassettes that rattle.

How do these artists earn a living? Partly by selling the tapes (don't reproduce them yourself—it's not nice), partly by schlepping from city to city, school to school on the low-budget form of the "celebrity" tour. There are obvious exceptions. Raffi, as elegant a performer as Fred Rogers, went promptly to gold. Hap ("Baby Songs") Palmer is comfortable. So is the group, Rosenshontz.

Then there are Doug Lipman, Bonnie Phipps, Joe Scruggs, Rory, Joanie Bartels, the Barolk Folk, and others who may or may not ever make big bucks but who are setting aesthetic standards for the coming generation of folktellers and minstrels.

Why are they doing what they are doing? Probably because they want to. Whatever their reasons, they are singing and telling our children about everything real—truth, beauty, heroes, rogues, courage, cowardice, wit, winsomeness, rivalry, wrath, laughter, and their opposites. They tell about balance too. And they do it with authenticity. Don't come to them for saccharine or second-rate. They and the following artists are masters, albeit of small canvases.

Beginning at the Beginning

A few days after your baby is born is not too soon to introduce music on cassette. After all, you've probably been singing to her or him for some time now. And now it will be exciting for you to watch the miraculous response. Don't push it, just begin slow and easy.

Connie Kaldor & Carmen Campagne

Lullaby Berceuse
Connie Kaldor & Carmen Campagne. Oak Street Music.
Cassette 2206. $9.95.   *Ages Birth–4.*

As lullaby tapes multiply, year after year, this one will remain in a position of preeminence, both for its thoughtful selection of songs and for the singers' strong loving voices that swaddle the listener and banish the cares of the day. Both the English-language side and the French combine traditional songs ("All through the Night," "Poulette Grise") with lovely new ones ("I Have You," "Petit Bebe"), all set against a gentle background of piano and guitar arrangements.

Earth Mother Lullabies from Around the World, Vol. 2
Pamala Ballingham. Earth Mother Productions.
Cassette 02 B. $7.50.   *Ages 1–5.*

Soprano Pamala Ballingham adopts a slow, deliberate tempo to reinforce the sleepy mood of this culturally diverse collection of ten lullabies. Her mellow singing, accompanied by gentle harp, flute, guitar, and keyboard arrangements, makes this fitting music for quiet times. The tape includes such familiar songs as the African-American "All the Pretty Little Horses" as well as unusual lullabies like "Hymn to a Moongoddess—A Hurrian Song from Ancient Ugarit."

Lullabies and Night Songs
Jan DeGaetani. Harper Audio. Cassette 1777. $9.95.   *Ages Birth–5.*

Alec Wilder's distinctive arrangements of tender, traditional lullabies and joyful night-songs celebrate day's end with laughter and delight. Included are "Go Tell Aunt Rhody," "Sea Lullaby," "Douglas Mountain," and "The Golux's Song."

Lullaby Magic
Morning Magic
Joanie Bartels. Discovery Music. Cassettes. $9.95 each.   *Ages Birth–6.*

Joanie Bartels sings with warmth and assurance. The first cassette, *Lullaby Magic,* offers a full, rich mix of contemporary and traditional lullabies, including James Taylor's "Close Your Eyes," the traditional "Rock-a-Bye-Baby," and Brahms's "Lullaby and Goodnight." The second tape is get-up-and-go-happily music, varying from Cat Stevens's "Morning Has Broken," and Lennon's "Good Day Sunshine" to such traditionals as "Lazy Mary Will You Get Up." The second side of both recordings is instrumental only, for singing along.

Hello Everybody
Rachel Buchman. Gentle Wind. Cassette 1038. $8.95.   *Ages 1–4.*

This friendly, comforting tape greets children at their own knee-high level.

Joanie Bartels

Many songs sound as if they began as affectionate bed-and-bath-time stories that were later elaborated upon. In one song Buchman hunts for body parts and takes little listeners on a tour of the anatomy. "Where's my elbow?" she says. "I've been looking for it all day." She combines original and traditional songs, which mainly take place in appealing home settings. There's just enough repetition to invite toddlers to join in.

Lullabies and Laughter

Pat Carfra. A & M Records of Canada, Ltd.
Cassette 2206. $13.
         Ages Birth–5.

Carfra's tone and mood are traditional, and her clear voice, with the "s-s-s" catch in it, has a removed comforting sound. Her choice of songs ranges from such lullabies as "Wynken, Blynken and Nod," based on Eugene Field's poem, to lively playsongs, including "Pop Goes the Weasel" on the second side.

Simple melodies, rhythms, and instrumentation have appeal for even the youngest children. It's the lyrics that make the difference. By two or three years old, little ones will begin to enjoy the humor, the fun puns, and the verbal gymboree of the songs listed below.

Hap Palmer

Animal Antics

Hap Palmer. Educational Activities. Cassette 604. $10.95.   ***Ages 2–5.***

The imitation of animal movement in exercise routines isn't new, but Hap Palmer's menagerie of monkeys, chickens, snakes, kitty cats, and other creatures offers young listeners both a physical and a mental workout. Lyrics crammed with such action words as *trundle, quiver, frolic, shrink, scuffle,* and *dart* help children visualize the distinct qualities of each animal's movements. Jazzy, original music sets the pace, which most youngsters will gleefully keep up with.

A House for Me

Fred Penner. Oak Street Music. Cassette. $9.95.   ***Ages 2–8.***

Using the text of Mary Ann Hoberman's picturebook *A House Is a House for Me,* Fred Penner creates a zippy song that kids tune into immediately—"A book is a house for a story/ a rose is a house for a smell/ my head is a house for a secret/ a secret I never will tell. . . ." This rich collection, set off by varied instrumentation, brings us other spirited numbers such as "Everything Is Tickety Poo" and "Crawdad." Here is great music from Canada.

Fred Penner

Down the Do-Re-Mi

Red Grammer. Children's Group.
Cassette 06847-84205-2. $9.98.   ***Ages 3–6.***

First and last, Red Grammer is fun, sweet fun. The timbre and strength of
his voice allow him to shift effortlessly from fast-paced silly ("The ABC's of
You") to tea-cosy cozy ("Dreamtime Rendezvous"). His carefully chosen
backups—from body slaps to banjo—and the voices of the children who
join him on many of the cuts combine to shape a sassy collection.

Circle Around

Tickle Tune Typhoon. Tickle Tune Typhoon Recordings.
Cassette 001. $8.98.   ***Ages 3–8.***

It's hard not to get caught up in the whirlwind of song and activity which
originates in live musical productions for children. The group is noteworthy for its original songs promoting diversity and acceptance. "Monster
Song" is delightfully gross, and it has a terrific message: It shouldn't matter
where you come from or what you look like. In another vein, "Vega Boogie"
celebrates such funky delicacies as Brussels sprouts, mustard greens, and
zucchini. This album—upbeat, caring, and fun—covers a lot of ground,
from Malvina Reynolds's number, "A Magic Penny," to the title song,
which comes from the Arapaho Indians.

Red Grammer

Doc Watson Sings Songs for Little Pickers

Doc Watson. Alcazar. Cassette 1005, $9. CD 1005D, $12.   ***Ages 4–7.***

Assembled both from live performances and archival materials, this tape
has remarkable consistency of sound. Watson's gravelly voiced introduc-
tions and his responsiveness to the audience give it the vitality and inti-
macy of a command performance. Harmonica, guitar, and "juice harp"
accompany the thirteen traditional songs, each sung in Doc's instantly
recognizable and uninhibited style.

Trying to separate story from music for children is sometimes silly—the
two go hand in hand, one enriching the other. Some of these ballads, tales,
and songs performed in conjunction with each other are irresistible.

Frog and Toad

Read by the author, Arnold Lobel. Listening Library.
2 cassettes 100. $15.95.   ***Ages 1–4.***

These green friends, Toad and the more stout-spirited Frog, make a quirky,
affectionate pair, and these vignettes frame some of the many ways two

friends can complement and protect each other. There's a hint of A. A. Milne's Eeyore in Toad, who glories sweetly in his miseries and needs to be walked through their solution by his friend, Frog. A dispirited child would find comfort in such tales. The narrator sounds as if he were comically imitating a more deep-voiced person, and the pretense effectively punctures any notion that the problems are at all serious.

Merry Christmas Strega Nona
Read by Celeste Holm. Six songs sung by Tom Glazer. Listening Library. Cassette 125CX, $9.95. Cassette and paperback 125SH, $14.95. **Ages 1–4.**

Celeste Holm's reading of *Strega Nona* has an exciting quality. Ornamented with seasonal flutey music, this recording of Tomie dePaola's book is filled with Christmas festivity. Strega Nona, or Grandma Witch, refuses to work her usual magic at this time of year because "Christmas has a magic of its own." Big Anthony, who is helping her prepare a great feast for the townspeople, allegedly forgets some crucial errands. But this being Christmas, miracles have a way of accomplishing themselves, and the townspeople provide Strega Nona with the feast she usually gives them. A delicate and important distinction is made between tricky magic and the magic of love.

Tell It with Me
Doug Lipman. A Gentle Wind. Cassette 1035. $8.95. **Ages 2–5.**

Doug Lipman is a storyteller who has a broad acquaintance with the many versions of any given tale. This knowledge is evident here. For instance, "The Tailor Who Felt Wonderful" is about a man who finds great happiness in a coat he made. When it's worn out, he finds equal happiness in the vest he makes from the remnants, and on down to the rag-end covering a button from the ultimate leftovers. What are finally, finally left are the story and its telling. Lipman's own stories and songs have the same kind of pedagogy and symbolism.

Girls and Boys, Come Out to Play!
Barolk Folk. Music for Little People. Cassette 2275, $9.98. CD D2275, $12.98. **Ages 3–6.**

This Mother Goose set to music ranges from familiar singing rhymes ("Do You Know the Muffin Man?" and "Lavender's Blue") to obscure seventeenth-century musical selections ("Adson's Masquing Ayre"). That the whole succeeds as a children's recording is testament to a knowledgeable selection of material and a commitment to using the familiar to introduce the unknown. The clear, pure voices of the singers and the traditional acoustic instruments (including recorders, treble viol, and dulcimer) create an exciting introduction to a period and style of music that might otherwise remain remote.

Chicka Chicka Boom Boom

Performed by Ray Charles. Simon & Schuster Books.
Cassette and hardcover 0-671-74894-7. $19.95.   *Ages 3–6.*

If ever a book required a rhythmic reading, it's this zany rhyming rendition of alphabetic antics. Side one of the tape has three versions of the text, the first two chanted by Ray Charles (one with and one without page-turning signals); the third, read by children, is rap style set to a hand-clapping beat. Side two begins with a sing-along version, followed by a brief chat with author John Archambault about how this silly rhyme came to be a book. Two final musical versions—one in reverse alphabetical order and one in soul style—complete an auditory extravaganza.

Norfolk Tales: Stories of Adventure, Humor and Suspense

Bobby Norfolk. Earwig Music. Cassette. $9.98.   *Ages 4–8.*

These adaptations of African and African-American tales use today's language, including street talk, to carry a universal message that has been true forever—place your faith in those who love you. The tales are well chosen and Norfolk's voice is an exciting instrument in the hands of a highly skilled performer. It soars and plummets, quavers and booms; it is every bit as captivating as the stories themselves.

Grandma Slid Down the Mountain

Cathy Fink and Friends. Rounder Records.
Cassette C8010, $9.50. CD, $15.   *Ages 5–10.*

The music is old-time country, folk, western swing, and rock 'n' roll. Cathy Fink and her talented friends blend superb musicianship and infectious enthusiasm to capture the imagination of young and old alike with this delightful collection of folk, camp, and story songs. Learn to yodel, to make peanut butter and jelly, a jazzy new way to enjoy "The Three Bears," what different moms do while their kids are at school, and just what *did* happen after the plate ran off with the spoon. A finger-snapping, toe-tapping pleasure.

Cathy Fink & Marcy
Marxer

A group of high-spirited recordings Just-for-the-Exquisite-Fun-of-It includes:

Mail Myself to You

John McCutcheon. Rounder Records.
Cassette C8016, $9.50. CD, $15. **Ages 3–5.**

An accomplished folk musician, John McCutcheon rouses any age audience with his exuberance. On this cassette, along with a chorus of children, he sings about the wonderfulness of animals and people. Traditional and contemporary material includes "Over in the Meadow," "Turn Around," and "The Awful Hilly Daddy-Willy Trip."

Tia's Dino-Stew Zoo

Tia's Quaker Tunes. Cassette. $9.95. **Ages 3–5.**

The wacky picture on the cover, showing Tia in an iridescent strapless gown caressing a dinosaur, hints at the playfulness to come. Tia leads the listener on a merry chase as she zips from language to language, style to style, playfully scooting down the alley of various musical feelings. Her constant companions are a group of giggling children, who sing well and who banter musically back and forth with her. The soulful, spirited musi-

John McCutcheon

Tia's Quaker Tunes

cal style that is Klezmer permeates a song about the guy of the hour—the dinosaur. But messages of peace, chorally proclaimed by kids and moved along by Tia, are also part of her picture.

Joe Scruggs

Deep in the Jungle

Joe Scruggs. Shadow Play Records & Video. Cassette. $9.95.   ***Ages 4–8.***

Beside containing some classic children's songs, this tape makes especially good use of "grown-up" musical styles—rock 'n' roll, some vocals reminiscent of the Andrews Sisters, and even a romantic ballad or two. Scruggs has a way with catchy novelty songs such as the clappy one that goes "Aunt Lucy had a baby/She named him Sherlock Holmes." And there's the one about a boy who buys his mother a skateboard. Even after you know the gimmick, you will laugh at this each time ("If she's not moving too fast/It's just because of the cast"). Scruggs sings affectionately about family themes, always in an upbeat beat.

On the Sunny Side

Maria Muldaur. Music for Little People.
Cassette 2222, $9.98. CD D2222, $12.98.   ***Ages 4–8.***

Maria Muldaur's voice projects part torch singer, part toddler. It has a baby-faced seductiveness that could easily miss the mark in a children's recording, but luckily doesn't. This collection of mostly familiar songs, from "Would You Like to Swing on a Star" to "On the Sunny Side of the Street," is dotted with lesser-known gems like "Never Swat a Fly." The one disappointment—a Dolly Parton sing-alike version of "Coat of Many Colors"—is more than made up for by the sweet duet sung by Muldaur and Amber McInnis in "Melancholy Baby." A diverse collection of ballads, lullabies, and comic songs.

Dinosaur Rock
Michele Valeri and Michael Stein. Harper Audio.
Cassette CP 1739. $11.   *Ages 5–10.*

Award-winning composer/performer Michele Valeri has joined with the talented instrumentalist Michael Stein to prove conclusively that dinosaurs may be extinct, but they are hardly forgotten. The humans tell the story of Professor Jones, paleontologist extraordinaire, who can temporarily yodel the dinosaurs back to life so that the animals can tell two curious children about Jurassic times. Songs range in style from rock 'n' roll to swing to bluegrass.

I Wuv You!
Bonnie Phipps. Children's Music Connection. Cassette. $10.   *Ages 5–11.*

Bonnie Phipps switches gears easily between rock, pop, jazz, and country-western. Her pacing is brisk and her sense of timing right. Plenty of fun sounds, musical variety, noises, and nonsense combine to create this mix. Among the inventive arrangements are the particularly catchy "Iko Iko" and "B, A, Bay."

Boogie! Boogie! Boogie!
Tom Pease. Tomorrow River Music. Cassette 8203. $9.95.   *Ages 5–11.*

Tom Pease, whose sound is always accessible and comfortable, sings such traditional songs as "Swinging on a Star" (with its famous chorus line "Or would you rather be a pig?"). Bluegrass, swing, jazz, and "family" rock establish the tone of the record. The title song offers a punning solution to the bogeyman problem: shout the words to a boogie-woogie beat, then dive under the covers.

Heather Bishop

A Duck in New York City

Heather Bishop. Oak Street Music. Cassette 027. $9.95.   ***Ages 6–10.***

In a series of very funny songs, a loquacious duck makes its way through
the Big Apple with the aid of vocalist Heather Bishop. Adventures abound
in tales about taxi drivers, robots, buffalos, slugs, and trees. A lyrical pot-
pourri set to engaging pop sounds, this tape captures the imagination and
tickles the funny bone.

Ethnic and heritage tapes are rooted in hope, laughter, tears, and, most
often, the protective love of one generation for the next.

Come Dance by the Ocean

Ella Jenkins. Smithsonian/Folkways.
Cassette 45014, $9. CD, $15.   ***Ages 3–6.***

Ella is ageless. In this all-new recording she works with groups of elementary and preschool children, as together they recite, chant, sing, repeat, and invent songs, games, and poems. Back and forth they go in a style that has become this artist's trademark. From "A Winter Plane Ride" to "A Solution to Pollution," these twenty-three selections sparkle with originality and warmth.

Mi Casa Es Su Casa/My House is Your House
Michele Valeri. Harper Audio. Cassette CPN 1708. $11.   ***Ages 3–8.***

Michele is an enthusiastic guide who leads young listeners on a tour of Latin countries. While her songs are original, they still incorporate the rhythms and folk themes of the countries visited. Even the very young can learn the Spanish words and phrases here, which are interspersed with lyricism and humor. This is a creative, joyful recording, painstakingly produced on a shoestring budget.

Shake It to the One That You Love the Best
Cheryl Warren Mattos. JTG of Nashville.
Cassette and book 4425. $15.95.   ***Ages 4–8.***

From the flip, sophisticated Miss in "Little Sally Walker" to her elderly— and slightly ridiculous—namesake in "Old Sally Wants to Jump," the characters in these play-songs and lullabies will appeal to children of many backgrounds. Clear, energetic vocals full of sly nuances plus spare but sprightly instrumentation, including everything from hand claps to alto sax, flavor this production. The many childhood favorites are drawn from the African-American tradition. The accompanying lyric book, with piano scores and brief explanations of the actions and/or origins of the songs, adds more than just words. It is beautifully illustrated with reproductions of work by Varnette P. Honeywood and Brenda Joysmith.

Canciones para el Recreo/Children's Songs for the Playground
Suni Paz. Smithsonian/Folkways. Cassette 45013, $9. CD, $15.   ***Ages 4–8.***

Viva Reissues! This 1977 rerelease is as welcome as a visit from an old and cherished friend. Suni Paz's bright clear voice swoops, trills, and hoots through these thirteen songs, which are sung in Spanish (there are printed English translations, five in meter for easy singing). Collected mostly from Chile and Argentina, they're full of the flavor and play of everyday life in those countries. Unusual instruments such as the ten-stringed Andean charango, the two-voiced bombo, and the rhythmic afuche provide energetic accompaniments and extend children's musical horizons.

Blow, Ye Winds, in the Morning:
A Revels Celebration of the Sea
Directed by John Langstaff. Revels, Inc. Cassette. $9.95.   ***All ages.***

From time immemorial the sea has inspired endless fascination that has found expression in chanteys, ballads, work songs, children's games, hymns, pub songs, and poetry. These have been recorded in live performance on this Revels release, which offers a rich blend of scholarship, artistic excellence, and celebratory spirit. The rousing chantey "A-Roving," which develops into a dock dance; the mournful "Mermaid," which warns of impending shipwreck; the work song "Pay Me My Money Down," with its strong hypnotic beat; and a poem by Walt Whitman are a few of the selections that will leave you with a taste of salt and a strong urge to run away to the sea.

Wassail! Wassail! An American Celebration of
the Winter Solstice
Directed by John Langstaff. Revels, Inc. Cassette. $9.95.   ***All ages.***

The variety of material presented on this recorded version of the Christmas Revels, held annually on the East and West coasts, is matched only by the diversity of talent assembled yearly to perform it. This one includes a full chorus, children, chicken chokers, Appalachian cloggers, a brass ensemble, Jean Ritchie, Robert J. Lurtsema, and many special instrumentalists. Here is music from the southern Appalachian Mountains, African-Americans, colonial New Englanders, the Shakers, and Native Americans. It is all artfully stitched together by prose and poetry selections into a luxurious quilt of American tradition.

Follow the Drinking Gourd
Read by Ron Richardson. American School Publishers.
Cassette and hardcover 909-691. $27.   ***Ages 7–9.***

The old spiritual—actually a set of directions for slaves to follow in escaping north to freedom—is woven around the story of Peg Leg Joe, a conductor on the Underground Railroad. Richardson's melodic voice gives full weight to the gripping narrative, and it brings to life the words of the compelling song, placing it squarely in the historic heart of America. Jeanette Winter's illustrations in the accompanying book are a bold modernization of folk-art-style primitives; the result is pictures with a contemporary as well as a "bygone" feel.

Widdecombe Fair
David Jones and Bill Shute. World Folk Arts.
Cassette 102. $9.50. **Ages 7–9.**

This music-hall-minus-the-sawdust production brings a taste of the British Isles right into the living room. The lead voice is deep and burry, the harmony vocals are as rich as fish stew, and the neatly picked guitar and banjo arrangements create a perfect background for sixteen ballads, work songs, and chanteys. Count along with "Old Tommy Nobbler," shudder happily at the variety of inventions made from "The Herring's Head," and cheer the hero's escape from the hangman's noose in the "Prickly Bush." This cassette, a treat for the family, is a glimpse of a large portion of our folk music heritage.

A Fish That's a Song
Smithsonian/Folkways.
Cassette and softcover C45037, $12.95. CD, $15.00. **Ages 7–12.**

This unique production combines folk art from the National Museum of American Art with recordings from the Smithsonian/Folkways archives, and the results are a mix of sampler, guided tour, and read-along. The audio portion is a who's who of American folk music—Pete Seeger, Woodie Guthrie, Doc Watson, Elizabeth Cotton, New Lost City Ramblers, and many others. As children listen to the music, their parents can point out connections with the art, which is reproduced in the accompanying thirty-eight-page booklet.

Why Mosquitoes Buzz in People's Ears
Performed by Bobby Norfolk. Earwig Music.
Cassette 4912C. $9.98. **Ages 8–11.**

Kids will want to imitate the growls and squeaks of Bobby Norfolk's highly original impersonations, which stamp his personality all over these stories—a combination of animated African folktales, southern black stories, and a few familiar classics. Hearing the erstwhile comedian prance with sound, listeners can almost see him vivaciously explain why mosquitos buzz in people's ears. It turns out the insect has been rejected for his part in a series of disasters and is doomed to rushing about asking nervously, "Is anybody still mad at me?" Norfolk also adds his own colloquial flavor to a hilarious retelling of the Wicked John story. "Have a nice day," he says sarcastically, both to St. Peter and to the devil.

Country Characters

Jackie Torrence. Earwig Music. Cassette 4909C. $9.98. *Ages 8–12.*

Jackie Torrence takes her listeners off into a world of eccentric characters—preachers, fiddlers, geezers, grumpy blacksmiths, even a sly and rather fetching devil. Their country ways and doings provide the backdrop for these ghost stories, which often tell of scotching death in return for living out some eerie ritual forever. For example, we hear of the dead playing prodigious music at a fiddling contest, and we see a dead brakeman glooming up and down the tracks, searching for his severed head. Torrence, a well-known storyteller, uses her extraordinary voice to wrap us into a deep spell punctuated with thrilling jolts of surprise.

Ghostly Tales of Japan

Rafe Martin. Yellow Moon Press.
Cassette 0-938756-23-0. $9.95. *Ages 10–up.*

This collection proves that children the world over love ghost tales. Young American listeners will be deliciously thrilled by familiar elements of the supernatural and by the exotic locales. "The Boy Who Drew Cats," for instance, tells of a young boy with a passion for sketching the animals. He persists in his efforts, despite the disapproval of his elders. However, in the end, his life is saved by the very cats that he drew, and the listener is reminded of the power of art and love.

Oy Chanukah!

Klezmer Conservatory Band. Rounder Records.
Cassette C3102, $9.50. CD, $15. *Ages 10–up.*

Oy Chanukah offers a rich tapestry of both Jewish lore and music. The record alternates between very spirited renditions of Klezmer music—a style that melds aching melancholy and a carnivallike joy—and spoken pieces. An older woman describes the celebration of Chanukah in a small *shtetl,* where the windows were illuminated with hundreds of candles; a little boy discusses *dreydls* (tops); another voice tells about Hannah and her seven sons, who were put to death because they would not renounce their religion. The variety of emotional lights and darks makes this cassette a moving explication of several aspects of Jewish life.

Then, wrapped in music and stories, are the messages that help shape sturdy morals and solid citizens.

Klezmer Conservatory Band

Peter Alsop

Take Me with You!

Peter Alsop. Moose School Records. Cassette 502. $10.   *Ages 5–8.*

This engaging record is somewhere between folky-friendly and early Beatles in feeling. Peter Alsop manages to combine singing (exuberant-sounding children accompany him) with some food-for-thought contemporary questions, which he puts in as little dialogues. Among other things, he raises issues, mostly unpompously, of peace, safety, sexual abuse, and parental expectations. He also deals with the inconsistency of children's wishes (too full for beans, but not for ice cream), as well as the foursquare logic parents use that sometimes misses the point.

Let's Help This Planet

Kim and Jerry Brodey. Children's Group.
Cassette and spiral-bound book 0-9695319-1-5. $15.   *Ages 5–9.*

From the paper that covers the songbook and cassette to the lyrics of the title song, every part of the album bespeaks this duo's respectful approach to the environment. Yet the message never overwhelms the music. Their voices dance up and down the scales in flawless, close-knit harmony; backup instrumentation is crisp and varied; songs are both singable and fun. In the midst of many environmentally correct lyrics, these shine forth like sun on a smog-free day.

I'm Just a Kid!

Rory. Sony Kids' Music. Cassette. $8.98.   *Ages 6–8.*

Beyond having a sweet voice and easy tone, Rory is genuine. In a collection of ten songs, one, "The Incredible Piglets," points kids to eat their veggies. Listening, one knows she cares about good nutrition, and knows she cares especially about kids. Another song, "The Ballad of Mr. Toad," deals with overcoming shyness. Rory's humor, verve, and warmth come through in every musical message she delivers, most particularly in the simple "The Best You Can Be Is You."

Evergreen Everblue

Raffi. MCA Records. Cassette 10060, $9.99. CD, $13.99.   *Ages 7–9.*

From whale song to scat singing, from rollick to rock 'n' roll, this is Raffi's ode to the environment. It's cautionary yet optimistic: we can preserve even as we progress, he says. His skill as a lyricist shines in "Mama's Kitchen"; his voice shows to greatest advantage on such old standards as

"One Light, One Sun." The production is as refreshing as pure water, as welcome as a clean breeze.

Bill Harley

Cool in School: Tales from the Sixth Grade

Bill Harley. Round River Records. Cassette, $10. CD, $15.   ***Ages 8–11.***

No matter how hard it is to be cool when you're ten or eleven, Bill Harley will make it better with his musicianship and his savvy stories about first love, homework, and the essence of cool. Using humor and heart along with rhythmic tunes, this maestro is in the fourth-, fifth-, and sixth-grade groove.

Real art and literature via CD and tapes? You betcha. Parents and grandparents who themselves enjoy listening and learning will want to try some of the following experiences with their families:

Waiting for Elijah

Judith Black. Yellow Moon Press. Cassette. $9.95.   ***Ages 5–11.***

Judith Black brings her exuberant reading to a collection of stories about

Passover. In "Miriam's Story" she uses the point of view of Moses' sister to relate the ancient Jews' flight from Egypt. Another tale, "The Fatal Pinch," tells of the anticipation and trepidation a child feels while waiting not only for the glorious Seder ceremony with its songs and meal, but also for the arrival of ebullient cheek-pinching relatives. "The Magician" is about a man who puts others before himself and who trusts that, at Passover, God will provide for him.

Classical Kids:
Beethoven Lives Upstairs

Beethoven Lives Upstairs
Performed by Stephen Ouimette and Nathaniel Moreau.
Classical Kids. Cassette CGN 2400. $8.98.   ***Ages 7–12.***

Christophe and his uncle exchange letters, and when a "madman" moves into the room above Christophe's, the boy writes of the event and those that follow. The unusual boarder is none other than the composer Ludwig van Beethoven, whom the boy comes to understand and even love. The story of the musician's unhappy childhood, his descent into deafness, and his struggles against this fate are unforgettably detailed. Interspersed among thirty-four musical excerpts is the youngster's sensitive view of the famous man's life.

Also recommended in the Classical Kids series: *Mr. Bach Comes to Call.*

The Life and Music of Johann Sebastian Bach
North Star, Cassette 0019. $9.95.   *Ages 7–12.*

Pique children's interests with *Mr. Bach Comes to Call* (Classical Kids), then
follow up with this chronological and more detailed account of his life.
Excerpts from several of his major works are included, among them "Jesu,
Joy of Man's Desiring," and a portion of a Brandenburg concerto.

Noah's Ark
Narrated by James Earl Jones. Penguin USA.
Cassette and hardcover 0-525-44525-0. $17.95.   *Ages 8–up.*

Actor James Earl Jones, composer Stewart Copeland, and illustrator Peter
Spier contributed to this cassette-and-book set which tells the story of
Noah and the Flood. Jones is imposing as the narrator. (Who, backed by a
rumble of thunder, could be better as the voice of God?) He reads two
versions of Noah's Ark. The first is a contemporary adaptation with a
pulsating musical score by Grammy Award–winner Copeland, drummer
for the former rock group The Police. We hear the animals, rain, lapping
water, creaking boards. Jones's second version is the traditional one from
the Book of Genesis. Either fits with Spier's picturebook, which won a
Caldecott Medal.

The Invisible Hunters
Read by Harriet Rohmer and Anna Olivarez. Children's Book Press.
Cassette, $8.95. Book 0-89239-036-0, $10.95.   *Ages 8–12.*

This legend, read in English and in Spanish, tells of three Miskito Indians
hunting in the Nicaraguan jungle who come across a sacred vine. The vine
promises to make them invisible if they vow never to use firearms or sell
their meat. The humans don't hesitate. Invisibility will help them track
animals; besides, the Miskitos freely give the fruits of their hunts to others
and use just sticks for weapons. Then, however, Europeans appear who
want to buy meat, and the hunters are sorely tempted. It is the old, sad
story of an aboriginal culture confronting Western civilization.

The Red Badge of Courage
Read by Richard Crenna. Durkin Hayes.
2 cassettes and book (abridged). $29.95.   *Ages 9–11.*

Stephen Crane's classic book about the Civil War is the story of a young
man's inner drama played out against the outer drama of the war. His early
thirst for the glory of battle undergoes a chastening and a transformation

into fear that he might lack the requisite courage actually to fight. Soon the character comes to recognize the compromising nature of that bloody badge he sought. Actor Richard Crenna uses a deep and craggy tone for the excited-action parts and a more contemplative one for the reflective parts. More than a war story, *The Red Badge of Courage* poetically explores the philosophical dialogue a soldier might have with his soldiering.

The People Could Fly

Read by James Earl Jones. Random House.
Cassette and hardcover 394-891-83X. $21.95.   ***Ages 9–up.***

These moving, exciting, and frightening stories from black folklore have been retold by Virginia Hamilton. Her book includes a glossary of the words in the Gullah dialect. (Gullah is a mixture of English, West Indian, and African.) Tape and book help each other through sometimes thick idiosyncratic poetry. Narrator James Earl Jones's voice is deep and portentous, his reading rich. The often supernatural tales of wily animals show tricksterism and some unsanitized evil. The title story tells the dream, expressed by some slaves, that by whispering certain ancient, secret African words to their companions, they can fly off into the air and away to freedom.

Tales of an October Moon

Marc Levitt. North Star. Cassette 0014/CS. $9.95.   ***Ages 10–up.***

Shiver city! Marc Levitt's deep dense voice is perfect for these truly original stories. In "The Little Skeleton Girl" the Tucker family reunion is ordinary except for one thing—it consists of skeletons. "The Old Man of the Stone Walls" and "The Purple Bishop" round out this haunting collection. Before you play it, build up the fire, turn down the lights, and lock all the doors.

Hell for a Picnic

Judith Black. Yellow Moon Press. Cassette. $9.95.   ***Ages 10–up.***

Anybody who would go to sea for no reason would go to hell for a picnic, say some folk. But the hero of this story has a good reason: years before, E. Michael Tarney's father, a sailor, left him in an orphanage. Father never came back, and the boy is desperate to find him. On the eve of the War of 1812, despite a crippled leg, the young man joins the crew of the USS *Constitution*—"Old Ironsides." Black's production re-creates life on the nineteenth-century warship in detail. Listeners hear the keening of gulls, the hiss of seaspray, and the moaning of the ship's planks; they virtually feel the vessel rolling underfoot. E. Michael encounters kindness as well as difficulty on his odyssey and the ending, while surprising, is happy.

Zlateh the Goat and Other Stories
Read by Theodore Bikel. Harper Audio.
Cassette CPN 1842. $9.95.   *Ages 10–up.*

Rich in Eastern European Jewish tradition and in humor, Isaac Bashevis Singer's collection of seven stories ranges from the silly to the sublime. In "The Mixed-up Feet" four silly sisters can't get up in the morning because they cannot untangle their intertwined appendages. In the title story the unswerving faithfulness of a farmer's most humble possession secures the spiritual as well as the physical redemption of both beast and master. Bikel's voice, rich, resonant, and expressive, infuses each word with life and casts these characters—from the fools of Chelm to the devil himself— as larger-than-life shadows of our imaginations.

The Island
Jay O'Callahan. Artana Records. Cassette A-12C. $10.   *Ages 10–up.*

In his ability to bring forth single-handedly a cast of characters and to set rich and complex scenes, storyteller Jay O'Callahan is nonpareil. Here he tells a tale of magic and adventure, which takes place on an island. In this story a battle between good and evil is played out by supernatural beings confronting their first humans. Vile Brinehart, with his malevolent fog, appears as do the monstrous creature Dardenelles and her mother, the Queen. The protagonist, a shipwreckee named Beals, learns about their ancient supernatural customs while they, in turn, learn what it is to be human.

Six Easy Steps to Choosing Audio Cassettes

1. Start with music and artists you enjoy.
Consider a Schubert lullaby or a Schumann cradle song, a Disney tune, Sweet Honey in the Rock's à cappella sound, a Pete Seeger melody, or Raffi himself. Your child will feel your pleasure and begin to get a sense of your standards.

2. Respect your child's developing interests.
For example, if he or she is fascinated by dinosaurs or by big machines, titles such as ***Dinosaurs Never Say Please*** (Bill Harley) or ***The Wheels of***

the Bus Go Round and Round will appeal. If weather is becoming an interest, a good possibility is *When the Rain Comes Down* (Cathy Fink).

3. Look for music and stories that reflect your child's heritage.
The Children of Selma (Rose Sanders), *I Know the Colors in the Rainbow,* or any other Ella Jenkins piece will appeal to all kinds of kids but African-American families may find them irresistible. *Latkes and Hamentashen* or *Mostly Matzo* (Fran Avni) are fun for all, though Jewish families might especially enjoy them. *Turkey in the Straw* (American Melody Records) offers traditional Americana.

4. Build your audio library with choices to suit different moods.
Quiet, reflective moments are enriched if a sensitive adult fits the right music or story to them. *Everybody Cries Sometimes* (Educational Activities) or the previously mentioned *Lullaby Magic* can be perfect. High-spirited moments will be enhanced by such titles as *In Search of the Wow Wow Wibble Woggle Wazzie Woodle WOO!* (Tim Noah) or, again, the unforgettable *Grandma Slid Down the Mountain.*

5. Choose recordings that help underscore your family's values.
Hug the Earth (Tickle Tune Typhoon) and *Rainbow Planet* (Rainbow Planet), for example, focus on the earth and on respect for people of all backgrounds.

6. Look for the Parents' Choice Foundation seal on the cassette package.
It means many other parents, children, and experts loved it.

Remember, Good Audio Cassettes:

- Stimulate imagination.
- Entertain and teach with first-class talent.
- Initiate and reinforce careful listening.

Equipment needed: A child's sturdy basic cassette player that is portable, inexpensive, and easy to repair.

5

Computer Programs

Computers are as much fun as cars used to be. They are available sooner—third grade is late—and they offer independence faster. "I can do it myself" quickly becomes, said or unsaid, "I can do it better than you"— fourth grade is late.

Born into a world of laser fiber optics, satellite communication, digital information, microchips, VCRs, CD ROMs, robotics, our babies have come a long way from the childhoods of their parents. Their world is as perplexing to most of their grandparents as grandys' own were to their immigrant forebears.

Now as then, it's thrillingly different, and frighteningly different.

Thrillingly different because this minute's events are available as they are happening anywhere and everywhere in the world. Thrillingly different because in well-equipped schools we have more and more access to all aspects of history—the most respected of the oldest and newest views of it— as on yet another window of the computer screen we watch it being made.

Our children and we, too, have become irreversibly linked to everyone else in our universe and, if we wish, to their backgrounds. The slightly befuddling Learning Resources and Technology Center is for our youngsters what the book-lined walls of the old library were for us. We may miss the soft sound and sachet scent of the librarian. They won't.

As the Dormouse said to Alice in Wonderland, "It's much of a muchness."

And it's frighteningly different for all of the same reasons, but especially because there is little time to gain perspective. This last particularly for adults who have historically used perspective to guide children.

Change—social, political, ethical, economic, technological—is the only constant.

In the tidiest of childhoods there is hardly reason for belief in continuity or solidity outside one's parents. That's for the lucky ones. Explanations of behavior beyond the children's own youth-beds, even their own walls, escape the wisest of their elders. Who can explain date rape or drive-by murder? For many families a race pace to the beat of "hurry-hurry" is standard. For some, the whirlwind is accompanied by something akin to emotional vertigo.

Where is the orderliness of Peter Rabbit's pastel world? Where can a kid find that safe comfort and get society's approval? For now there's no place where one step logically follows the next as consistently as it does in a good computer program. Good computer programs don't glorify violence, drugs, or too-soon sex, and *they're cool.*

Here you can eighty-six the rush. There's time to think, and no need to feel . . . at least not the frenzy.

The following computer programs won't let your kids down.

PLEASE NOTE: *The appropriate age for these programs is, in this category perhaps more than in any other, dependent on the child's interests and skills. Experts' and publishers' suggestions are less exact than your own and, as she or he gets older, than your child's.*

For the Youngest

Among the most enticing programs for two- and three-year-olds are those bright in color and mood. They can feature animated characters playing and learning. Shapes, comparative sizes, object identification, numbers, and letters keep baby hackers interested. The following programs seem to satisfy their requirements and ignite their enthusiasm to learn more.

McGee
Lawrence Productions. IBM, Macintosh, $24.95.
Apple IIGS, $39.95. Mouse required. *Ages 2–6.*

Preschoolers will enjoy the sights and sounds of this program, in which McGee, a toddler of indeterminate sex, wakes before his mother and explores their six-room house—alone. Using voice commands or a mouse, the real child clicks on a small picture of a place or object and McGee performs a related action there. He might pick up a toy in his room, walk

McGee

into a hallway, or modestly close the bathroom door. Some scenes contain spoken dialogue or other sound effects, like the splashing sounds in the bathroom. This playful program entertains youngsters and familiarizes them with the computer.

McGee at the Fun Fair

Lawrence Productions. IBM, Macintosh, $24.95.
Apple IIGS, $39.95. Mouse required.   *Ages 2–5.*

The sequel to McGee has all the virtues of the original: children can use it independently, since reading skills are unnecessary; the setting is pleasantly familiar; and the program combines animation, speech, and sound effects. This time McGee and his family go to the summer fun fair in the park. As children click on one of four small pictures, McGee will watch a juggler, climb on the monkey bars, listen to a one-person band, or explore other vistas. When this becomes too tame, parents can use one of the suggestions from the manual.

The Playroom

Broderbund Software. IBM, $44.95.
Macintosh with color monitor, $49.95. Apple II series, $39.95.   *Ages 2–4.*

Preschoolers can enter this playroom without their parents and play with all the different toys. When they select a toy, they start an animated

The Playroom

sequence that samples many subject areas. If they click on the clock, for instance, players see both an analog and a digital face. They also see where the sun is and what happens at that time of day. Other toys include a board game and a spinner game, an ABC book, and a mixup toy that provides a matching activity. It's all tempting fun as little ones learn and practice reading readiness, ABCs, and 1, 2, 3's.

Mickey's ABC's

Mickey's 1 2 3's

Mickey's Shapes and Colors
Walt Disney Computer Software. IBM, $39.95 each.
Recommended sound source, $34.95 extra. *Ages 3–6.*

If you get only one, get Mickey's ABC's, a tempting blend of text, sight, and sound. When children type a letter, Mickey wakes up and gets involved with an object beginning with that letter. Press *J*, for instance, and Mickey gets juice; press *F*, and he goes to the fair. Both the letter and the word appear on the screen, and both are pronounced by the computer. Curiosity may drive parents to tap a few letters themselves, just to see what happens.

Although it's fun to play with, Mickey's 1 2 3's is sometimes confusing. Children type a number and then that number of objects appears on the screen. However, since the art is two-dimensional, when wheels on cars or trucks are displayed, not every wheel actually appears. The car, for instance, shows only two of its four wheels. Objects being counted occasionally appear onscreen from right to left and this may disconcert children who are just learning to read from left to right.

Children too young to recognize letters may enjoy Mickey's Shapes and Colors. But first, an older person must install a plastic cover over the keyboard. This cover contains shapes and colors, which children press to activate the screen. Children who have already used a keyboard may find the cover unsettling, but newcomers to the computer will feel right at home.

Talking Math and Me
Davidson and Associates. Apple, $49.95. *Ages 3–6.*

In twelve different learning games this entertaining program introduces early math. Using a mouse or keyboard, your child might match shapes, match objects with numbers, select number sequences, or compare "more than" and "less than." Animated monkeys plus a variety of sound effects keep the mood light. Two tries, both wrong, and the program pops out the right answer. Kids who want to can print out certificates for themselves or color the accompanying activity book.

Amanda Stories: Inigo

Amanda Stories: Your Faithful Camel Goes to the North Pole
Voyager Company. Macintosh, $24.95 each.
CD ROM, $54.95 (both). *Ages 3–up.*

A mischievous cat named Inigo is the main character in the first program, a series of four adventure stories. Children click the mouse to control the action—to turn a page, for instance, or call up a whale who might take Inigo for an underwater ride. The stories offer choices so children have alternatives as they play Inigo again and again.

For those partial to camels, a trip to the North Pole may be in order. The second program, like Amanda's cat tales, is long on whimsy. All the stories are so clever and well drawn that children may notice their parents lurking about, hoping to catch a glimpse of the action.

Stars and Planets
Advanced Ideas. Apple IIGS, IBM, $44.95. *Ages 3–6.*

Six games are set in outer space, and each introduces basic prereading skills through imaginative play. Children count, for example, by helping an astronaut collect the number of moon rocks shown on the lunar lander. The ship leaves only when the correct number has been selected. Kids also build rockets, name planets, and practice other basic skills such as matching shapes, colors, sizes, sequencing, and letter recognition.

Picture Chompers

MECC. Apple with color monitor, $59. *Ages 4–6.*

Giant teeth chomp on every right answer a player makes in this imaginative classification game. Identify objects according to size, color, design, or use and the Big Teeth may even gobble them up. Miss and the teeth crack. The program seems like a video game without violence but actually it's a drill (no pun intended) for math and reading skills.

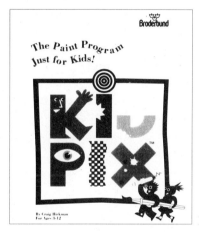
Kid Pix

Kid Pix

Broderbund Software. Macintosh, IBM, $59.95. *Ages 4–7.*

An imaginative design program, Kid Pix is absorbing. You can arrange enticing graphics by selecting from an array of pictorial choices. Use the options to change the screen in unexpected ways. There are 100 "rubber stamps," an Electric Mixer tool for really special effects, and a clown that acts as a wild card. Hidden pictures can be uncovered with a special eraser. Unexpectedly amusing sounds—such as "oops" when you choose to "undo" —add to the fun. Features include a second voice naming the letters in Spanish. A Small Kids Mode keeps the youngest artists from blundering into older kids' turf.

Ages Five to Eight

From about five years through eight the subjects of the best computer programs reflect your child's broadening interests. Time is a new concept; the minutes and hours of the day, the days of the week, the months and seasons of the year are becoming an understandable part of life. Reading is a sharp challenge. Going to the store with an adult or, on occasion, without one, demands arithmetic skills. There are animals to find out about, classifications to establish, labels to give things, and, all around, the earth to treasure.

Reader Rabbit I
Learning Company. IBM with color monitor, $49.95.
Macintosh, Apple, $59.95.   *Ages 5–8.*
Reader Rabbit's pleasant tone and some excellent color graphics combine to create an early reading, spelling, and vocabulary program that coaches as it entertains. Reader Rabbit clearly pronounces more than two hundred three-letter words, which are categorized into such groups as "Travel" (bus, jet) and "Containers" (bag, net). Children can use either a keyboard or a joystick to play any of the four games. One is a sorting activity, one involves labeling, one focuses on differences between similar words, and one is a matching game. Games get progressively more difficult, and a dancing rabbit cheerfully applauds every right answer.

Talking Classroom
Orange Cherry Software. Apple IIGS, $49.   *Ages 4–7.*
Point the mouse at a clock and hear a human voice tell what time it is . . . aim at a globe and find out the names of the continents . . . hit a computer key and its name is spoken. An Art Corner lets kids paint by mouse, changing colors at will; the Calendar teaches names of the days of the week; and a Money Poster shows and tells money equivalents. Here's an entertaining introduction to school for the younger children in this age group; for the older ones, it's a nifty review.

Talking First Reader
Orange Cherry Software. Apple IIGS, $49.   *Ages 4–8.*
When a human-sounding computer asks children to find the word *dog*, it seems like a game. And when the children do spell *dog* correctly and then the dog barks, they're encouraged to keep going. The three games in this

program help beginning readers get plenty of practice in a lighthearted atmosphere. In one they hear a word and select the written word that matches a pictured object. In another they complete a simple sentence. And in the third they read an entire sentence about a picture. When children read longer material, a bouncing ball helps them target each word.

Woolly Bounce

MECC. Apple, $59.   *Ages 5–7.*

What happens if you drop a bowling ball from a height of ten wooden blocks? Will it bounce more times on a hard surface than a soft one? What about a golf ball? This program encourages a spirit of scientific inquiry by allowing children to alter variables at will. An easy, positive approach to beginning physics, the program is meant to be integrated with ongoing observation. Youngsters won't need a manual or worksheets to pick up the two main messages: asking questions is integral to science, and many factors influence the way *any* ball bounces.

Easy Street

Mindplay. Apple, Macintosh, IBM, $49.99.   *Ages 4–8.*

With this program, playing "store" has entered the computer age. Children create shopping lists, which appear on the screen in words and pictures. Then the black belt shoppers, or shoposauruses, wander through stores matching each shop's wares against the lists. On the next level, they learn to make purchases and to make change. As shoppers wend their way along Easy Street they get practice with letters, numbers, and patterns. Zany touches, including Knuckles the Gorilla, keep the learning atmosphere light.

Math Rabbit

Learning Company. Macintosh, $59.95.
Apple II series, Apple IIGS, IBM, $39.95.   *Ages 5–7.*

Imaginative and multisensory, these arithmetic games are light-years away from dreary drills as Math Rabbit takes over from Reader Rabbit. In the Clown's Counting Game players make music by moving up and down a numbered scale. In the Mystery Matching Game they match pairs of objects, numbers, or even problems. More than two dozen different options make this an adaptable program with an unwaveringly good-humored emcee.

Balancing Bear

Sunburst Communications. Apple II series, IBM, $65.   *Ages 5–8.*

Balancing Bear has a scale. Children try to keep it even by adding or subtracting numbered weights. As they do, they see the math concept known as equivalence. Games start simply and can get progressively harder; numbers get higher and more weights are required. Visual clues and spirited hints help children succeed. Incorrect answers are never penalized. This approach, coupled with clear, simple graphics and language, encourages playfulness with numbers, which continues in Subtract with Balancing Bear.

Learn About Animals

Sunburst Communications. Apple II series, IBM, $65.   *Ages 5–7.*

Children match a fox with its den and then get to watch the animal curl up for a snooze. They match a snake to its food and get to watch it swallow a lizard. While these animal lovers learn what some eat, they are also learning about counting, matching, classifying, measuring, and comparing. Later, players can move on to more creative activities.

Jungle Safari

Orange Cherry Software.
Macintosh, Apple IIGS, CD ROM, $59.   *Ages 5–8.*

A jeep or a boat takes youngsters through plains, prairies, rivers, and rain forests. Kids see the sights and hear sounds. As the explorers see an animal that interests them, they can push a button to learn more about it—its name, its habits, its young. Besides the usual lions and monkeys, youngsters also meet dik-diks, goliath beetles, and other exotic creatures.

Stickybear Word Scramble

Weekly Reader Software/Optimum Resource.
IBM (except IBM PC Jr.), $49.95.   *Ages 6–10.*

Before Stickybear can begin to solve the word puzzles, he must first dodge spheres and collect floating stars for energy. Then he—and the children who control him—can choose among several word games presented with arcade-type graphics. Players get to unscramble words, find listed words hidden in a grid, or play a concentration-type memory matching game. If children ever tire of these, players (or their parents) can enter new word lists to create new games.

LEVEL ■5 SCORE ■2550 Stickybear Word Scramble

Math Shop Jr.

Scholastic Family Software. Apple IIe, Apple IIGS, IBM, $69.95.
Macintosh, $79.95. **Ages 6–9.**

In this shopping game all the players are clerks who work in one of a mall's
nine shops. They make change, they load bags equally, or they fill prescrip-
tions using, of course, the correct combination of ingredients. Besides
supplying lots of practice in street-smart math, this program shows kids
the real-life application of academic skills.

BannerMania

Broderbund Software. Apple II series, IBM, $34.95.
Macintosh, $59.95. **Ages 6–9.**

Great big splashy words, if you want, in a variety of wonderful designs,
shapes, and fonts are yours for the making. Try out combinations galore.
Create numerous banners, flags, insignia, signs, bumper stickers, birthday
cards. Choose from among fifty ready-made banners, forty designs, twenty-
seven shapes, twenty special effects such as 3-D shadows, and nineteen
fonts. GRAMMA IS FIFTY-SIX YEARS OLD TODAY! FIDO HAS LARYNGITIS.
MR. JONAS WEARS RED UNDERWEAR.

New Math Blaster Plus!

Davidson & Associates. Macintosh, Apple II series, $59.95.
IBM, $49.95. **Ages 6–11.**

Four different arcade-type games, complete with animation and space-age

BannerMania

sound effects, amuse math fans and phobics while they learn to solve problems and make the techniques their own. In one game, as they clean up space trash with laser beams, youngsters find the missing values in equations. Six different difficulty levels help them succeed. The game format not only reduces math anxiety, but also helps develop critical thinking. In Alge-Blaster Plus older players use graphing skills to defend their space station from asteroids. The teaching M.O. is the same—set up an intriguing problem, demonstrate a way to solve it, and let the users proceed at their own pace and pleasure.

Ages Eight to Ten and Up

At this age life is becoming multifaceted. A growing range of subjects is acquiring some depth. Girls and boys still want toys and yet they know in their hearts it's time to let go of them. The prepubescent are a frisky lot, and a varied one. Some at nine, ten, and eleven still have worms in their pockets; some are young adults eager to see, do, touch, possess, or share in everything and still get their parents' approval. Here are some programs that have appealed to them.

PC USA

P. C. Globe. IBM, $49.95. *Ages 8–up.*

Kids who like zeroing in on such things can call up maps, geographic features, major cities, or data ranging from a state's history to the number of schools per child in the community to how many robberies occur— on the average—per hour. They can compute distances between cities, help themselves or others in virtually every subject, and, while they know themselves for eggheads, have fun.

Paper Plane Pilot

MECC. Apple, $59. *Ages 8–12.*

Budding scientists and paper plane aficionados will enjoy fiddling with this interactive simulation. They'll discover how four variables—plane shape, weight, launcher angle, and launcher force—affect the distances a paper plane will travel. They'll make test flights and observe, collect data, and make predictions based on information (as all *good* scientists do). While they're at it they'll review the laws of gravity, motion, and force. And they'll be flying.

Call the Parrot

Hartley Courseware.
Apple II series, Macintosh with 2e emulator, $49.95. *Ages 8–10.*

Starting with a map of an island, where a pirate has buried his treasure, players proceed step by step in this treasure hunt. Over the terrain they go, encountering everything from King Kong's pinky ring to temple ruins. They must keep an eye out for the parrot, which always tells the truth, and the pirate, who always lies.

Because the treasure is buried in a different place each time—and because the layout of the island is different each time—users must exert logic, memory, and directional skills to win the game.

Super Solvers: Midnight Rescue

Learning Company. IBM, $49.95. Macintosh, $59.95. *Ages 8–11.*

Before midnight, sleuths must discover which robot is actually Morty Maxwell, master of mischief, in disguise. If they fail, Morty will paint the school with disappearing paint. To collect a clue, read a short passage and then answer questions. The graphics are exciting, from the endless labyrinth of rooms and stairwells to the victory dance (performed by either your super solver or a robot, depending on how successful you were).

Backyard Birds
MECC. Apple II, $59.   *Ages 9–12.*

If you think bird-watching is for nerds, you haven't played Backyard Birds. Here are more than twelve hundred North American feathered vertebrates. Look at one, record your observations, then, fast, try to identify the particular bird before it flies away. Do it again. And again.

Multiply with Balancing Bear
Sunburst Communications. Apple II series, $65.   *Ages 9–11.*

Once again, Balancing Bear presents the glamorous equivalents—this time in multiplication. Using bright balloons, each a different price, he gives pedagogy pizzazz. Just pick out equivalent equations, such as four twelve-cent balloons and eight six-cent ones, and, ha! you've balanced the balloons in the bear's hands. The screen does what no ordinary worksheet can do—visually demonstrates the relationships between numbers. The program has three levels of difficulty, and an excellent adult guide.

Crosscountry USA
Didatech. Apple II, IBM, $49.   *Ages 9–14.*

Put your kids in the driver's seat. They can work individually or in teams, as truck drivers who must locate their cargoes—anything from apples to zinc. The truckers must determine the shortest route, calculate their expenses, and navigate varied terrain. Planning pays off, because the truckers will encounter real-life problems: finding the best food, buying gasoline, and dealing with mechanical difficulties. Whew! No one will get bored on this trip.

Lunar Greenhouse
MECC. Apple II series, $59.   *Ages 8–12.*

The assignment is growing food for a moon colony. The goal is to get the best possible yield in the shortest amount of time. Young horticulturalists can set and adjust such variables as light, water, and temperature. They gauge their results by pressing the "grow" button and keeping one eye on their maturing plants and the other eye on the calendar, which ticks off dozens of days in a few seconds. Budding scientists will be reminded of the rewards of careful observation, comparison, and learning from mistakes.

However, adults might want to point out that real life and science require time that simulation doesn't.

Where in the World Is Carmen San Diego?

Where in the World Is Carmen San Diego?

Broderbund Software. Macintosh, IBM, $49.95.

Apple II series, Commodore, $35.95.   ***Ages 10–up.***

As almost everybody knows, Carmen is a "quadruple agent for so many countries that even she has forgotten which one she is working for." Your first assignment is to stalk and capture her nasty crew of bandits—felonious undesirables like Merey LaRoc, the free-lance aerobic dancer. To do this will require globetrotting, picking up clues, and using the crime-lab computer. Good luck, Rookie!

Your second assignment, O Experienced One who's become hooked on Carmen, is to find out Where in Time Is Carmen Sandiego? and then Where in America's Past Is Carmen Sandiego? These, and the other programs in the series, add extra dimensions as the peripatetic baddie keeps running.

Whales!

Top Ten Software. Apple II series, IBM, $49.95.   ***Ages 10–up.***

Players aboard the *Mary Clyde* are wildlife explorers. They are trackers on the trail of different species, using old skills (observation) and modern ones (satellite tracking). In other adventures on the program, players try to

Where in America's Past Is
Carmen Sandiego?

discover a whaling captain's ancient secrets, rescue a stranded whale, and defend whale habitats. It's all riveting adventure.

Some children, in school and out, are now coming closer and closer to adult thinking and skills. Their dexterity with the computer and their delight in their own mastery are a joy for them and their parents no matter how many times either says, "Aw, shucks, 'tain't nuthin'."

Bushbuck: Global Treasure Hunter

P. C. Globe. IBM, $39.95. *Ages 10–up.*

You have five weird items to hunt down—possibilities include a hat made from fungus, a snowshoe, and a bottle of Dead Sea mud. You are given the name of the city to which each item must be returned. Now fly to various spots on the globe and collect clues (learning geography along the way). Go alone, with or against a buddy, or compete with Pierre, the electronic henchman.

SimEarth

Maxis. IBM with DOS 3.0 and up, Macintosh,
IBM with Windows, Amiga, $69.95. ***Ages 10–up.***

What if you created a planet of your own? What if you could control it from its beginnings to its end ten billion years later? Heady stuff—and SimEarth gives you your chance to influence continental drift, form and destroy continents, raise world temperatures with the greenhouse effect, or lower it with cloud formations and rainfall. Express yourself—supervise or create intelligent life forms (even civilized dinosaurs or genteel carnivorous ferns) and guide them through the complex interactions of your planet's ecosystem. But keep your head—if you don't watch out, you might get flashing messages of mass extinctions occurring.

Hidden Agenda

Scholastic Family Software. Macintosh, IBM, $99.95. ***Ages 12–up.***

Coups and crises abound in this exploration of Central American history and politics. The player becomes president of a mythological country for three years and faces a term of decisions. Food and cash shortages and disgruntled military are only some of the problems. Almost any course of action the president takes will make someone in the diverse population unhappy. At the end of the term, the player is given an article from a future encyclopedia delivering the "verdict" of history. However, only the player can decide if the game has been won or lost.

Exploring Tidepools

WINGS for Learning.
Apple II series (with color monitor), $75. ***Ages 9–15.***

Begin by investigating tidepools on the rocky Central California coast, to see how the pools are covered and uncovered by the tide and how different kinds of life survive at different depths and exposure times. You can choose to look underwater or watch things under a microscope. Next you'll have a chance at tidal cycles, plankton cycles, "who eats whom," and the difference between East Coast and West Coast tidepools. An enclosed field guide helps explain it all.

Guidelines to Choosing Computer Programs
for Young Children

A good computer program has a clear purpose. It is sharply focused; it is a challenge and a pleasure to use.

A good computer program must:

- Capture your child's attention with bright colors, deft animation, energetic sounds, or captivating characters.
- Fit your child's abilities and, as her or his skills increase, expand to fit them.
- Provide clear instructions.
- Respond promptly (fast feedback).
- Correct errors and explain them.

The best programs for your child will excite her or his interests. They will:

- Provide a variety of formats that repeat the same information in various ways.
- Sharpen motivation with rewards.
- Include a sense of play, humor, triumph, or delight.

6

Magazines

THE BASIC CONCEPTS of periodicals—that there is more to know about almost every subject and that visions and revisions in all fields are ongoing, considerable, often exciting—stimulate flexibility and open-mindedness. Beyond this the medium implies that finding out takes time. That there's a time-consuming perseverance necessary in the making of a maven is a truth genuinely tough for 1990s children to comprehend. After all, they know only this barrage-of-information age and therefore have every reason to believe real news does come in sight and sound bytes. Everything you need to know, someone will give you fast.

For kids, one of the unavoidable conclusions triggered by reading magazines is that there's a full and fascinating world "beyond mine." Old-fashioned as the magazine genre may be, the information's cool.

Children who see magazines regularly often experience the pleasure of discovering "new" facts and fictions on their own. It is at this point that real growing-up growth begins. Heady it is; it's also hard.

But competence never did come cheap. Competence requires a great deal of the family, more than ever. It requires moms and dads who can accept their children's choices and passions, not the other way around. After that it's just a question of the children's finding the right references, allowing themselves to enjoy, learn, and then practice. And practice. And practice some more.

Did Julius Erving do less? Or Dr. Salk or Jackie Joyner-Kersee or YoYo Ma?

But they, like children, need "take-in" time. Not chill-out-to-TV time, though that too can be a help, but time to stop giving and start getting— getting information that nurtures the mind easily or poetry that does the same for the soul. This, too, is in the magazines that come through the mail "for me."

From the alphabet to anthropology it's available in children's magazines, in the library, or for home use by subscription.

The following magazines are listed in age appropriate order. All are recommended. We suggest, however, that like adults, children can be inundated with too much reading, making it a chore rather than a pleasure.

Choose magazines on the basis of your child's emerging or established interests.

Preschool—Primary

Chickadee
Young Naturalist Foundation. $20.33/10 issues.   *Ages 3–8.*

Families interested in the natural sciences and particularly in animals will enjoy introducing youngsters to the fine nonfiction, photography, illustration, and just-for-fun information in these remarkably varied pages.

Ladybug
Carus Publishing. $29.97/12 issues.   *Ages 2–7.*

High-quality stories, poems, and illustrations are accompanied by puzzles, a simple cartoon strip, and games. The mood of the periodical is gentle, the tone traditional. Like its older sister publication, *Cricket, Ladybug*'s pulse beats to a literary drummer.

Sesame Street Magazine
Children's Television Workshop. $16.97/10 issues.   *Ages 2–6.*

As up-to-the-minute and visually interesting as the TV show it is based on, this preschoolers' periodical introduces numbers and reading readiness. Because no actual reading is required, little ones are often able to peruse the magazine on their own.

Primary—Elementary

American Girl
Pleasant Company. $19.95/6 issues.   *Ages 7–12.*

For those girls who are not interested in becoming teenagers before their time, this slick publication, an offshoot of the best-selling American Girl Book and Doll series, was established in 1992. Lavishly designed, its contents have a personalized historical slant: i.e., "What was it like to be a girl in ——?" The mixture of historical fiction, nonfiction, and activities is solid.

Cricket

Carus Publishing. $29.97/12 issues.   ***Ages 6–14.***

Children who enjoy the finest literature will devour the short stories, poems, and masterful art in this elegant publication. The most renowned writers and illustrators in contemporary children's books contribute to it with clear pleasure.

Hopscotch

The Bluffton News Publishing & Printing Co. $15./6 issues.   ***Ages 6–12.***

A delightful periodical, this one is aimed at girls. They are the protagonists in the fiction and nonfiction stories and articles. Current and historical women set rigorous standards for young females. A number of crafts and activity-related articles are included.

Kidsports

Proserv Publishing. $9.97/6 issues.   ***Ages 7–14.***

A colorful 8 × 11 bimonthly, this magazine presents straightforward instruction and motivation. "Here's how" is its first credo; "Do it" is its second. Advice, written in a lively style, is given by well-known coaches. Try a newsstand copy before subscribing to the advertising-rich magazine.

Sports Illustrated for Kids

Time Warner. $18.95/12 issues.   ***Ages 7–12.***

From its inception, the junior edition of the best-selling adult magazine has been exactly what it seems—colorful, readable, and a hit, particularly with sports-minded reluctant and not-so-reluctant readers.

Intermediate—Older

Cobblestone

Cobblestone Publishing. $22.95.   ***Ages 8–12.***

The history magazine for children examines a different timely subject in each issue. The antislavery movement, railroad trains, and Hispanic children are some examples of a substantial and accessible route to learning. *Cobblestone* shows and tells us what, where, and who we were.

Faces

Cobblestone Publishing. $17.95.   *Ages 9–15.*

People and cultures over the world are highlighted and examined in high caliber nonfiction articles. As in other Cobblestone publications each issue has a theme; photographs or reproductions of paintings or sculpture enrich the subject matter. Anthropology for youngsters? Maybe it's unprecedented, but it works—the magazine has a devoted following.

Kids Discover

Kids Discover. $14.95/10 issues.   *Ages 8–12.*

A glossy magazine, this one takes a single subject in each issue and engagingly covers many, many aspects and facets of it. One outstanding issue dealt with bubbles, another with pyramids. The articles, plus its do-it-yourself projects and photographs, have heavy-duty child appeal. Note that the publisher's age recommendation begins at age six. We suggest that children from eight to twelve will enjoy more pleasure and less frustration.

National Geographic World

National Geographic Society. $12.95/12 issues.   *Ages 8–12.*

Highly respected, the junior edition of its long-lived parent, *National Geographic,* contains games, jokes, activities, art, and mail from readers. In addition to the superb nature photos and features there are strong, but never intimidating, profiles of kids who courageously follow their own interests and integrity.

Odyssey

Cobblestone Publishing. $19.95/10 issues.   *Ages 8–15.*

If your child shows a determined interest in hard science or natural science, there is no finer magazine for her or him. Well-written, factually correct articles are interspersed with handsome photographs; the subjects are varied, ranging from this world to others in an impressive series of issues. There is not a whiff of patronizing from the distinguished authors.

3-2-1 Contact

Children's Television Workshop. $16.97/10 issues.   *Ages 8–12.*

Any kids' magazine with this one's address—its actual location is on the

Square, more precisely at E = MC Square—is clearly aimed at the bright and the fun-loving, those kids with a slight academic bent. Every brazenly colored page brims with odd bits of eclectic information. Based on the excellent PBS show of the same name, the mag is aimed at children who've cut their reading teeth on *Sesame Street* and the not quite so well-focused *Kid City.*

Zillions (formerly Penny Power)
Consumer Reports For Kids. $16./6 issues.   **Ages 7–14.**

"A fool and her (or his) money are soon parted," goes the old saying. Yet children who read this consumer publication learn more about nickel, dime, and dollar value more quickly than adults will believe. Articles and design are unfailingly interesting; the layout has panache and practicality.

Other magazines of interest you may want to examine in your local library: *Calliope; Child Life; Highlights; Humpty Dumpty; Ranger Rick; Owl; Jack and Jill.*

For young writers there are the outstanding student-written *Stone Soup* (Children's Art Foundation), *Merlyn's Pen,* and *Shoe Tree.*

Magazines available in braille or large print are *Boys' Life, Children's Digest,* and *Jack and Jill.* A few others are offered on audio cassette for the visually impaired.

Addresses for Magazines

American Girl
The Pleasant Company
8400 Fairway Place
Middleton, WI 53562-0998

Boys' Life
Dept. S202
P.O. Box 152079
Irving, TX 75015-2079

Calliope
Cobblestone Publishing
7 School St.
Peterborough, NH 03458
603-924-7209
$17.95 / 5 issues.

Chickadee
Young Naturalist Foundation
56 The Esplanade, Ste. 302
Toronto, ONT M5E 1A7, CANADA
416-868-6001
$20.33 / 10 issues.

Child Life
1100 Waterway Blvd.
P.O. Box 567
Indianapolis, IN 46206

Children's Digest
1100 Waterway Blvd.
P.O. Box 567
Indianapolis, IN 46206

Cobblestone
Cobblestone Publishing
7 School St.
Peterborough, NH 03458
603-924-7209
$22.95 / 10 issues.

Cricket
Carus Publishing
Subscription Dept.
P.O. Box 52961
Boulder, CO 80332
800-888-6995
$29.97 / 12 issues.

Current Science (classroom)
Field Publications
245 Long Hill Rd.
Middletown, CT 06457
203-638-2638
$6.95 / 18 issues.

Dolphin Log
Cousteau Society
870 Greenbrier Cir., Ste. 402
Chesapeake, VA 23320
804-523-9335
$10.00 / 6 issues.

Dynamath (classroom)
Scholastic Magazines Inc.
P.O. Box 3710
Jefferson City, MO 65102
800-631-1586
$6.50 / 8 issues.

Faces
Cobblestone Publishing
7 School St.
Peterborough, NH 03458
603-924-7209
$17.95 / 9 issues.

Highlights for Children
803 Church St.
Homesdale, PA 18431

Hopscotch
P.O. Box 1292
Saratoga Springs, NY 12866

Humpty Dumpty Magazine
1100 Waterway Blvd.
P.O. Box 567
Indianapolis, IN 46206

Jack and Jill
P.O. Box 567
Indianapolis, IN 46206

Kids Discover
170 Fifth Ave.
New York, NY 10010

KidSports
ProServ, Inc.
1101 Wilson Blvd.
Arlington, VA 22209

Ladybug
Carus Publishing
Subscription Dept.
P.O. Box 58342
Boulder, CO 80322
800-888-6995
$29.97 / 12 issues.

Merlyn's Pen
(by children for children)
P.O. Box 1058
East Greenwich, RI 02818

National Geographic WORLD
National Geographic Society
Washington, DC 20036
202-857-7000
$12.95 / 12 issues.

Owl
Young Naturalist Foundation
56 The Esplanade, Ste. 304
Toronto, ONT M5E 1A7, CANADA
416-868-6001
$20.33 / 10 issues.

**Ranger Rick Magazine /
Nat. Wildlife Federation**
8925 Leesburg Pike
Vienna, VA 22184-0001

Sesame Street Magazine
Children's Television Workshop
P.O. Box 55518
Boulder, CO 80322
800-678-0613
$16.97 / 10 issues.

Shoe Tree (by children for children)
P.O. Box 452
Belvidere, NJ 07823

Sports Illustrated for Kids
P.O. Box 830609
Birmingham, AL 35283

Stone Soup
Children's Art Foundation
P.O. Box 83
Santa Cruz, CA 95063
800-447-4569
$23.00 / 5 issues.

Super Science Blue (classroom)
Scholastic Magazines Inc.
P.O. Box 3710
Jefferson City, MO 65102
800-631-1586
$6.50 / 8 issues.

3-2-1 Contact
P.O. Box 53051
Boulder, CO 80322

Zillions (formerly **Penny Power**)
Consumers' Union
Subscription Dept.
P.O. Box 51777
Boulder, CO 80323-1777
800-234-2078
$16.00 / 6 issues.

Bibliography and Suggestions for Further Reading

Books

Bianculli, David. *Teleliteracy.* New York: Continuum, 1992.

Blank, Marion, and Laura Berlin. *The Parents' Guide to Educational Software.* Redmond, Wash.: Tempus Books, 1991.

Boehm, Helen. *The Right Toys: A Guide to Selecting the Best Toys for Children.* New York: Bantam, 1986.

Braiman-Lipson, Judy, and Deborah Fineblaum Raub. *Toy Buying Guide.* Mount Vernon, N.Y.: Consumer Reports Books, 1988.

Dewing, Martha. *Beyond TV: Activities for Using Video with Children.* Santa Barbara: ABC-CLIO, 1992.

Graves, Ruth, ed. *The RIF Guide to Encouraging Young Readers.* New York: Doubleday, 1987.

Green, Diana Huss, ed. *Parents' Choice Magazine Guide to Video-Cassettes for Children.* Mount Vernon, N.Y.: Consumer Reports Books, 1989.

Hearne, Betsy. *Choosing Books for Children: A Commonsense Guide.* New York: Doubleday, 1990.

Jarnow, Jill. *All Ears: How to Choose and Use Recorded Music for Children.* New York: Penguin, 1991.

Katz, Bill, and Linda Sternberg Katz. *Magazines for Young People.* New Providence, N.J.: R.R. Bowker, 1991.

Kelley, Marguerite. *The Mother's Almanac II.* New York: Doubleday, 1989.

Larrick, Nancy. *A Parent's Guide to Children's Reading.* 5th ed. New York: Bantam Books, 1983.

Lipson, Eden Ross. *The New York Times Parents' Guide to the Best Books for Children.* New York: Random House, 1991.

Lurie, Alison. *Don't Tell the Grown-Ups: Subversive Children's Literature.* Boston: Little, Brown, 1990.

Neil, Shirley Boes, and George W. Neil. *Only the Best: The Annual Guide to Highest-Rated Educational Software.* New Providence, N.J.: R.R. Bowker.

Oppenheim, Joanne. *Buy Me Buy Me: The Bank Street Guide to Choosing Toys For Children.* New York: Pantheon, 1987.

Richardson, Selma K. *Magazines for Children: A Guide for Parents, Teachers and Librarians.* Chicago, American Library Association, 1991.

Trelease, Jim. *The New Read Aloud Handbook.* New York: Penguin, 1989.

Wager, Debbie, and Judy Nygren. *Good Toys: Parents' Guide to Toys and Games.* Bethesda, Md.: National Press Inc., 1986.

Periodicals

Book Links. Chicago: American Library Association.
BookList. Chicago: American Library Association.
The Horn Book. Boston: Horn Book.
Parents' Choice. Newton, MA 02168: Parents' Choice Foundation.
Sightlines. Chicago: American Film and Video Association.
Video Librarian. Bremerton, WA 98310

Pamphlets

Chang, Margaret A. *The Chinese Experience: China and Chinese Americans.* Children's Book Bag, Foundation for Children's Books.
Ringquist, Lois. *Rainbow Collection: Multicultural Books for Children.* Minneapolis Public Library.

If You Can't Find It in the Stores, Try These Catalogs

Mostly Toys

Animal Town
Animal Town
Box 485
Healdsburg, Calif. 95448
800-445-8642

Back To Basic Toys
Back To Basic Toys
8802 Monard Dr.
Silver Spring, Md. 20910
800-356-5360

Childswork/Childsplay
Alternative Toy Co.
441 N. Fifth St., 3rd Fl.
Philadelphia, Pa. 19123
800-962-1141

Constructive Playthings
Constructive Playthings
1227 E. 119th St.
Grandview, Mo. 64030
800-255-6124

Creative Publications
Creative Publications
5040 W. 111th St.
Oak Lawn, Ill. 60453
800-624-0822

Dale Seymour Publications
Dale Seymour Publications
P.O. Box 10888

Palo Alto, Calif. 94303
800-USA-1100
(in Calif.: 800-ABC-0766)

Discovery Corner Catalogue
Lawrence Hall of Science
University of California
Berkeley, Calif. 94720
415-642-1016

HearthSong
HearthSong
P.O. Box B
Sebastopol, Calif. 95473
800-325-2502

PlayFair Toys
PlayFair Toys
P.O. Box 18210
Boulder, Colo. 80308-8210
800-824-7255

The Right Start
The Right Start
5334 Sterling Center Dr.
Westlake Village, Calif. 91361
800-548-8531

Safari Ltd.
Safari Ltd.
P.O. Box 630685
Miami, Fla. 33163
800-554-5414

Toys To Grow On
Toys To Grow On
2695 E. Dominguez St.
P.O. Box 17
Long Beach, Calif. 90801
800-542-8338

Mostly Books

Brown Sugar and Spice
Brown Sugar and Spice
8584 Whiteharn
Romulus, Mich. 48174
213-729-0501

A Child's Collection
A Child's Collection
155 Avenue of the Americas
New York, N.Y. 10013
212-691-7266

Chinaberry Book Service
Chinaberry Book Service
2830 Via Orange Way
Spring Valley, Calif. 92708-1521
800-776-2242

GTC
Gifted Child
P.O. Box 6448
Mobile, Ala. 36660
800-476-8711

The Heritage Key
The Heritage Key
10116 Scoville Ave.
Sunland, Calif. 91040
818-951-1438

Nasco Learning Fun
Nasco Learning Fun
901 Janesville Ave.
Fort Atkinson, Wis. 53538
800-558-9595

Telltales
Telltales
P.O. Box 277
Woolrich, Maine 04579-0277
800-922-READ

Mostly Computer Software

Broderbund Software
Broderbund Software
17 Paul Dr.
San Rafael, Calif. 94913-2947
800-521-6263

Family Software
Family Software
915 Elmwood Ave.
Evanston, Ill. 60202
312-475-2556

Macintosh Educational
Software Collection
Chariot Software Group
3659 India St., Ste. 100C
San Diego, Calif. 92103
800-298-CHARIOT

Mindplay
Mindplay
P.O. Box 36491
Tucson, Ariz. 85716
800-221-7911

Mostly Audio Recordings

Children's Small Press Collection
Children's Small Press
719 N. Fourth Ave.
Ann Arbor, Mich. 48104
313-668-8056

Educational Activities
Educational Activities
P.O. Box 87
Baldwin, N.Y. 11510
516-223-4666

Family Music
Enrichment Resources
Box 427
Pembroke, Mass. 02359
617-294-8228

A Gentle Wind
A Gentle Wind
Box 0391
Albany, N.Y. 12203
518-436-0391

Kiddie Cat
Alcazar
P.O. Box 429
Waterbury, Vt. 05676
802-244-8657

Kimbo Educational
Kimbo Educational
P.O. Box 477 E
Long Branch, N.J. 07740
201-229-4949

Ladyslipper
Ladyslipper
P.O. Box 3130
Durham, N.C. 27705

Linden Tree
Linden Tree
170 State St.
Los Altos, Calif. 94022
415-949-3390

Listening Library/Bookmates
Listening Library/Bookmates
1 Park Ave.
Old Greenwich, Conn. 06870
800-243-4504

Music for Little People
Music for Little People
P.O. Box 1460
Redway, Calif. 95560
800-346-4445

Music in Motion
Music in Motion
Box 5564
Richardson, Tex. 75080
800-445-0649

Miscellaneous

Beckely Cardy Quarterly
Beckely Cardy
1 E. First St.
Deluth, Minn. 55802
800-227-1178

Edmark
Edmark
6727 185 Ave. NE
Redmond, Wash. 98052
800-426-0856

Kapable Kids
Kapable Kids
80-9 Knickerbocker
Bohemia, N.Y. 11716
800-356-1564

One Step Ahead
One Step Ahead
151 Pfingspen
Deerfield, Ill. 60015
800-274-8440

Indexes

I. Index by Category

Books

Videos

Audios

Computer Programs

Magazines

II. Index by Age

Except for toys, all ages suggested here are rough guidelines only. They indicate the years when the largest number of children will reap the most benefit from the book, video, audio, or computer program. While more specific ages are suggested on each review, the key here, as everywhere, is *know your child.*

Recommended ages are always inexact calls. They suggest the time period most children fully enjoy the product. Our headings are Infants, Toddlers, Preschool, Primary, Intermediate, and, in some cases, Older.

Age Index Toys

Infants
Ages Birth–1 ¹/₂

Activity Walker, 8
Baby Mirror, 2
Bag 'n' Train, 3–4
Circus Musical Mobile, 2
Clutch Mirror, 2
Domino Babies Musical Mobile, 2
Double Feature, 2
Little Red Ride-On, 3
Rock-a-Stack, 3
Shiny Rattle Assortment, 2
Skwish Classic, 2–3
Spinning Rattle, 2
Spring-a-Ling, 8–10
Tot Mobile, 2
Twin Rattle Teether, 2

Toddlers
Ages 1–2 ¹/₂

Activity Walker, 8
Baby's First Train, 5–6
Bag 'n' Train, 3–4
Dr. Drew's Discovery Blocks, 6

Duplo Building Sets, 6
Fuzzy Puzzle, 5
Hugg-a-Planet: Earth, 16
Little Red Ride-On, 3
Lotsa Blocks, 6
Mega Blocks 40 Piece Set, 7
Neat New Toy, 4–5
1-2-3 Bike, 10
1-2-3 Family House, 14
Puzzle Truck, 13–14
Rock-a-Stack, 3
Sand and Water Activity Table, 13
Skwish Classic, 2–3
Spring-a-Ling, 8–10
Toddler Tractor and Cart, 8
Toddle Tots Family House, 14

Preschool
Ages 3–5

Activity Gym, 14
Around the World Hat Box, 12
Basic Build 'n' Store Chest, 6
Big Dump Truck/Big Loader, 15
BRIO-Mec sets, 7
Career Hat Box, 12
Chimalong, 15

Primary
Ages 6–8

Intermediate
Ages 9–11

Age Index Video

Ages Beginning at 10 months

Ages 2–4

Intermediate
Ages 9–11

Older
Ages 12–up

Age Index Computer Programs

If you have a computer at home you may begin teaching two-year-olds who show interest in learning. The programs that follow are set up in years, not cognitive age groupings.

PLEASE NOTE: *The appropriate age for these programs is, in this category perhaps more than in any other, dependent on the child's interests and skills. Experts' and publishers' suggestions are less exact than your own and, as she or he gets older, than your child's.*

Ages 2–up

Ages 3–up

Age Index Magazines

III. Book Index by Author, Editor, and Illustrator

IV. Index of Composers and Audio Recording Artists

V. Index of Companies

Company Addresses

A&M Video
1416 No. Labrea
Hollywood, Calif. 90028
213-469-2411

A&M Records of Canada, Ltd.
1345 Denison St.
Markham, Ontario
CANADA L3R 5V2
416-752-7191

ABC School Supplies
Box 4750
Norcross, Ga. 30091
800-669-4222

Advanced Ideas
591 Redwood Highway, Ste. 2325
Mill Valley, Calif. 94941
510-526-9100

AIMS Media
9710 De Soto Ave.
Chatsworth, Calif. 91311-4409
800-637-3469

Alcazar
P.O. Box 429
Waterbury, Vt. 05676-0429
800-541-9904

American Melody Records
Box 270
Guilford, Conn. 06437
203-457-0881

American School Publishers
P.O. Box 5380
Chicago, Ill. 60680
800-843-8855

Anatex Enterprises
15929 Arminta St.
Van Nuys, Calif. 91406
800-999-9599

Aristoplay
P.O. Box 7028
Ann Arbor, Mich. 48107
800-634-7738

Artana Records
P.O. Box 1054
Marshfield, Mass. 02050
617-837-0962

Atheneum
866 Third Ave.
New York, N.Y. 10022
212-702-2000

Avon Camelot
1350 Avenue of the Americas
New York, N.Y. 10019
212-261-6800

Backos Game Company
8527 Norborne
Dearborn Heights, Mich. 48127
313-563-0235

Barr Films
P.O. Box 7878
Irwindale, Calif. 91706-7878
800-234-7879

Battat
P.O. Box 1264
Plattsburg, N.Y. 12901
518-562-2200

Beckley Cardy Catalog
One East 1st St.
Deluth, Minn. 55802
800-446-1477

Bluffton News Publishing & Printing
(Hopscotch)
P.O. Box 164
Bluffton, Ohio 45817
419-358-4610

Bradbury
866 Third Ave.
New York, N.Y. 10022
212-702-9809

BRIO Scanditoy
655 West Mill Rd.
Milwaukee, Wis. 53218
800-558-6863

Brock Optical
P.O. Box 940831
Maitland, Fla. 32794-0831
800-780-9111

Broderbund Software
P.O. Box 6125
Novato, Calif. 94948-6125
800-521-6263

Bullfrog Films
P.O. Box 149

Oley, Penn. 19547
800-543-FROG

Candlewick Press
2067 Massachusetts Ave.
Cambridge, Mass. 02140
617-661-3330

Carolrhoda
241 First Ave. North
Minneapolis, Minn. 55401
612-332-3344

Carus Publishing
Subscription Department
P.O. Box 58342
Boulder, Colo. 80322
800-BUG PALS

CBS/FOX
1330 Avenue of the Americas
Fifth Floor
New York, N.Y. 10019
800-800-aFOX

CC Studios
Weston, Conn. 06883
800-KIDS-VID

Century Products
9600 Valley View Rd.
Macedonia, Ohio 44056
216-468-2000

Children's Art Foundation
P.O. Box 83
Santa Cruz, Calif. 95063
800-447-4569

Children's Book Press
6400 Hollis St., Ste. 4
Emeryville, Calif. 94608
510-655-3395

Children's Circle
Division of Weston Woods
CC Studios Inc.
Weston, Conn. 06883
800-KIDS-VID

Children's Group
Children's Book Store Distributors
67 Wall St., Ste. 2411
New York, N.Y. 10005
800-668-0242

Children's International Network
2580 NW Upshur #202
Portland, Ore. 97210
800-677-7607

Children's Music Connection
P.O. Box 9656
Denver, Colo. 80209
800-395-6791

Children's Television Consortium
1333 Gough St., 8 M.
San Francisco, Calif. 94110
800-359-9000 ext. 814

Children's Television Workshop
One Lincoln Plaza
New York, N.Y. 10023
212-595-3456

Children's Television Workshop
Subscription Department
P.O. Box 52000
Boulder, Colo. 80321-2000
800-678-0613

Chronicle
275 Fifth St.
San Francisco, Calif. 94103
800-722-6657

Churchill Films
12210 Nebraska Ave.
Los Angeles, Calif. 90025
800-334-7830

Clarion Books
215 Park Ave. South
New York, N.Y. 10009
212-420-5800

Classical Kids
134 Howland St.
Toronto, Ontario
Canada M54 3B5
800-668-0242

Cobblestone Publishing
7 School St.
Peterborough, N.H. 03548
800-821-0115

Community Playthings
P.O. Box 901
Rifton, N.Y. 12471-0901
800-777-4244

Concept Video
P.O. Box 30408
Bethesda, Md. 20824
800-333-8252

Consumer Reports for Kids
Subscription Department
P.O. Box 51777
Boulder, Colo. 80323-1777
800-234-2078

Cornerstone Books
P.O. Box 388
Arnold, MO 63010-0388

Cousteau Society
870 Greenbrier Cir., Ste. 402
Chesapeake, Va. 23320
804-523-9335

Creativity For Kids
Creative Arts Activities
1600 E. 23rd St.
Cleveland, Ohio 44114
216-589-4800

Crown
225 Park Ave. South
New York, N.Y. 10003
212-254-1600

Dakin
1649 Adrian Rd.
Burlingame, Calif. 94010
415-692-1555

Davidson and Associates
19850 Pioneer Ave.
Torrance, Calif. 90503
800-556-6141

Delacorte
666 Fifth Ave.
New York, N.Y. 10103
212-765-6500

Dell (Bantam Books)
1540 Broadway
New York, NY 10036
212-782-6500

Dial
375 Hudson St.
New York, N.Y. 10014
212-366-2800

Didatech Software
3812 Williams St.
Burnaby, British Columbia
Canada V5C 3H9
800-665-0667

Discovery Music
5554 Calhoun Ave.
Van Nuys, Calif. 91401
800-451-5175

Disney Home Video
500 South Buena Vista St.
Burbank, Calif. 91521-7145
800-72-Disney

Dr. Drew
P.O. Box 510501
Melbourne Beach, Fla. 32951
407-984-1018

Durkin Hayes Publishing
One Colomba Dr.
Niagra Falls, N.Y. 14305
716-298-5150

Dutton
375 Hudson St.
New York, N.Y. 10014
212-366-2000

Earth Mother Productions
P.O. Box 43204
Tuscon, Ariz. 85733
602-575-5114
800-788-6543

Earwig Music
1818 West Pratt Boul.
Chicago, Ill. 60626
312-528-5455

Editoria Patria
Sade CV Canoa 591
60 Piso
Colonia Tizapan
San Angel, MEXICO 01090

Educational Activities
P.O. Box 392
Freeport, N.Y. 11520
800-645-3739

Educational Insights
19560 South Rancho Way
Dominquez Hills, Calif. 90220
800-933-3277

Educo International
123 Cree Rd.
Sherwood Park, Alberta
Canada T8A 3X9
800-326-TOYS

Elkind & Sweet/Live Wire Video
Live Wire Video
3315 Sacramento St.
San Francisco, Calif. 94118
415-564-9500

European Toy Collection
6643 Melton Rd.
Portage, Ind. 46368
219-763-3234

Evans
216 E. 49th St.
New York, N.Y. 10017
800-462-6420

Family Games
P.O. Box 97
Snowden, Montreal
Canada H3X 3T3
514-485-1834

Family Home Entertainment
P.O. Box 10124
Van Nuys, Calif. 91410
818-778-3823

Farrar, Straus and Giroux
19 Union Square West
New York, N.Y. 10003
212-741-6900

Field Publications
245 Long Hill Rd.
Middletown, Conn. 06457
203-638-2638

Fisher-Price
636 Girard Ave.
East Aurora, N.Y. 14052
800-432-5437

Folkmanis
The Enchanted Forest Catalog
85 Mercer St.
New York, N.Y. 10012
800-456-4449

Games Gang
2720 W. 28th St.
P.O. Box 1429
Pine Bluff, Ariz. 71603
800-558-3291

Gentle Wind
Box 3101
Albany, N.Y. 12203-0103
518-436-0391

Gulliver
1250 Sixth Ave.
San Diego, Calif. 92101
619-699-6810

Green Tiger Press
Simon & Schuster
200 Old Tappan Rd.
Old Tappan, N.J. 07675
800-223-2336

Greenwillow
1350 Avenue of the Americas
New York, N.Y. 10019
212-261-6500

Growing Child
P.O. Box 620
22 No. 2nd St.
Lafayette, Ind. 47902
317-432-2624

Harcourt Brace Jovanovich
1250 Sixth Ave.
San Diego, Calif. 92101
619-699-6810

HarperCollins, Harper Trophy
10 E. 53rd St.
New York, N.Y. 10022
212-207-7044

Harper Audio
P.O. Box 588
Dunmore, Penn. 18512
800-331-3761

Hartley Courseware
133 Bridge St.
Dimondale, Mich. 48821
517-646-6458

Henry Holt
115 W. 18th St.
New York, N.Y. 10011
212-886-9200

Heros/Darda
1600 Union Ave.
Baltimore, Md. 21211
800-638-1470

Hi-Tops/Media Home Entertainment
5730 Buckingham Way

Culver City, Calif. 90230
213-216-7900

Holiday House
425 Madison Ave.
New York, N.Y. 10017
212-688-0085

Houghton Mifflin
Two Park St.
Boston, Mass. 02108
617-725-5000

Hugg-a-Planet
247 Rockingstone Ave.
Larchmont, N.Y. 10538
800-332-7840

Human Relations Media
175 Tompkins Ave.
Pleasantville, N.Y. 10570-9973
800-431-2050

Intempo Toys
P.O. Box 50157
38 Erstwild Court
Palo Alto, Calif. 94303
800-326-TOYS

Intervideo Association
174 Lake View Ave.
Cambridge, Mass. 02138
617-661-6843

Joy Street (now Little, Brown)
41 Mt. Vernon St.
Boston, Mass. 02108
617-227-0730

JTG of Nashville
1024-C 18th Ave. South
Nashville, Tenn. 37212
800-222-2584

Jugglebug
7506-J Olympic View Dr.
Edmonds, Wash. 98026
800-523-1776

Kids Discover
P.O. Box 54205
Boulder, Colo. 80332
800-284-8276

Kidvidz
618 Centre St.
Newton, Mass. 02158
800-637-6772

Kinderworks
P.O. Box 1441
Portsmouth, N.H. 03801
603-692-2777

Knopf
225 Park Ave. South
New York, N.Y. 10003
212-254-1600

Krafty Kids
11358 Aurora Ave.
Des Moines, Iowa 50322-7907
515-276-8325

La Fête Productions
225 Rue Roy East
Bureau 203
Montreal, Quebec
CANADA 90749
514-848-1471

Lakeshore Learning Center
P.O. Box 6261
Carson, Calif. 90749
310-537-8600

Lancit Media
601 W. 50th St.
Sixth Floor
New York, N.Y. 10019
800-358-5858

Lawrence Productions
1800 So. 35th St.
P.O. Box 458
Galesburg, Mich. 49053
616-665-7075

Learning Company
6493 Kaiser Dr.
Fremont, Calif. 94555
800-852-2255

Lego
Shop At Home Services
P.O. Box 1310
Enfield, Conn. 06083
800-527-8339

Lights, Camera, Interaction!
578 Post Rd East, Ste. 520
Westport, Conn. 06880
203-222-7529

Lightyear Productions
350 Fifth Ave., Ste. 5101
New York, NY 10018
212-563-4610

Listening Library
One Park Ave.
P.O. Box 611
Old Greenwich, Conn. 06870
800-243-4505

Little Tikes
2180 Barlow Rd.
Hudson, Ohio 44236
216-650-3000

Little, Brown
34 Beacon St.
Boston, Mass. 02108
617-227-0730

Lodestar Books
375 Hudson St.
New York, N.Y. 10014
212-366-2627

Lothrop, Lee and Shephard
1350 Avenue of the Americas
New York, N.Y. 10019
212-261-6641

Lotsa Blocks
630 Hickman Dr.
Sauk Centre, Minn. 56378
612-352-3372

McElderry Books
966 Third Ave.
New York, N.Y. 10022
212-702-7855

Macmillan Publishing
866 Third Ave.
New York, NY 10022

Marlon
P.O. Box 1530
Long Island City, N.Y. 11101
718-361-2088

Maxis
2 Theatre Square, Ste. 230
Orinda, Calif. 94563-3346
510-254-9700

MCA Home Video
70 Universal City Plaza
Universal City, Calif. 91608
818-985-3894

MCA Records
70 Universal City Plaza
Universal City, Calif. 91608
818-777-4000

MECC
6160 Summit Dr.
Minneapolis, Minn. 55430-4003
800-685-MECC

Meccano
888 Seventh Ave., 30th Fl.
New York, N.Y. 10106
212-397-0711

MGM/UA Home Video
10000 W. Washington
Culver City, Calif.
213-280-6000

Michael Sporn Animation
632 Broadway, 4th Fl.
New York, N.Y. 10012
212-228-3372

Mindplay
3130 N. Dodge Boul.
Tuscon, AZ 95716
800-221-7911

Miramar Productions
200 2nd Ave. West
Seattle, Wash. 98004
800-245-6472

Moose School Records
P.O. Box 960
Orinda, Calif. 94563-3346
800-676-5480

Morrow
1350 Avenue of the Americas
New York, N.Y. 10019
212-261-6691

MPI Home Video/ABC News
15825 Rob Roy Rd.
Oak Forest, Ill. 60452
800-323-0442

Mulberry
1350 Avenue of the Americas
New York, N.Y. 10019
212-261-6691

Music For Little People
Box 1460
Redway, Calif. 95560
800-346-4445

National Geographic Society
Educational Services
17th & M St. NW
Washington, D.C. 20036
800-821-0115

New Line Home Video
Columbia Tristar Home Video
    Distribution
3400 Riverside
Burbank, Calif. 91505-4627
818-972-8090

North Star
95 Hathaway St.
Providence, R.I. 02907
401-785-8400

Oak Street Music
93 Lombard Ave., Ste. 108
Winnipeg, Manitoba
Canada R3B 3B1
204-957-0085

Orange Cherry Software
Box 390 Westchester Ave.
Pound Ridge, N.Y. 10576
914-764-4104

Orchard
387 Park Ave. South
New York, N.Y. 10016
212-686-7070

Pappa Geppetto's Toys
Victoria Limited
Box 81
Victoria, British Columbia
V8W 24M CANADA

Paramount Home Video
5555 Melrose, Ste. 309
Los Angeles, Calif. 90038
213-468-5526

P. C. Globe
4440 Rural Rd.
Tempe, Ariz. 85282
800-255-2789

Penguin USA
375 Hudson St.
New York, N.Y. 10014
212-366-2000

Philomel Books
200 Madison Ave.
New York, N.Y. 10016
212-366-8700

Phoenix/BFA Films and Video
468 Park Ave. South
New York, N.Y. 10016
212-366-8700

Playmobil USA
11-E Nicholas Ct.
Dayton, N.J. 08810
908-274-0101

Playskool
P.O. Box 200
Pawtucket, R.I. 02863-0200
800-PLAYSKL

Pleasant Company
8400 Fairway Pl.
Middleton, Wis. 53562-0190
800-845-0005

Poppets
908 Eighth Ave.
Seattle, Wash. 98109
800-241-1161

Proserv Publishing
Kidsports
P.O. Box 55497
Boulder, Colo. 80322
800-388-1266

Public Media Video
5547 N. Ravenswood Ave.
Chicago, Ill. 60640
800-826-3456

Puffin
1350 Avenue of the Americas
New York, N.Y. 10019
212-261-6500

Putnam
200 Madison Ave.
New York, N.Y. 10016
212-951-8700

Rabbit Ears Productions
distributed by UNI
5 S. Sylvan Rd.
Westport, Conn. 06880
203-857-3760

Rainbow Planet
5110 Cromwell Dr.
Gig Harbor, Wash. 98335
206-265-3758

Random House
225 Park Ave. South
New York, N.Y. 10003
212-254-1600

Random House Home Video
400 Hanh Rd.
Westminster, Md. 21157
800-733-3000

Ravensburger/International
   Playthings
120 Riverdale Rd.
Riverdale, N.J. 07457
800-631-1272

RCA Columbia
See Sony.

Revels, Inc.
One Kendall Square, Bldg. 600
Cambridge, Mass. 02139
617-621-0505

Rhyme and Reason Toys
232 W. Exchange St.
Providence, R.I. 02903
401-272-8369

Ritvik
760 Lepine Ave.
Dorval, Quebec
Canada H9P-1G2

Round River Records
301 Jacob St.
Seekonk, Mass. 02771
508-336-9703

Rounder Records (Roundup)
P.O. Box 154
North Cambridge, Mass. 02140
800-44-DISCS

Scholastic
730 Broadway
New York, N.Y. 10003
212-505-3000

Scholastic Family Software
P.O. Box 7502
Jefferson City, Mo. 65102
800-631-1586

Sesame Street Home Video
Children's Television Workshop
1 Lincoln Plaza
New York, NY 10023
212-595-3456

Shadow Play Records & Video
P.O. Box 180476
Austin, Tex. 78718
800-274-8804

Simon & Schuster Books
200 Old Tappan Rd.
Old Tappen, N.J. 07675
800-274-8804

Smarty Pants
15104 Detroit Ave., Ste. 2
Lakewood, Ohio 44107
216-221-5300

Smithsonian/Folkways
One Camp St.
Cambridge, Mass. 02140
800-346-4445

Sony Kids' Music
550 Madison Ave., 21st Floor

New York, N.Y. 10101
212-833-4231

Sony Kids' Video
1700 Broadway
New York, N.Y. 10019
212-689-8897

Sunburst Communications
101 Castleton St.
Pleasantville, N.Y. 10570
800-628-8897

T. C. Timber/Habermaass
P.O. Box 42
Skaneateles, N.Y. 10570
800-468-6873

Telephone "Doctor"
12119 Charles Rock Rd.
Saint Louis, Mo. 63044
314-291-1012

Tensegrity Systems
1362 Route 9
Tivoli, N.Y. 12583
800-227-2316

Tia's Quaker Tunes
P.O. Box 1363
Mercer Island, Wash. 98040
206-568-9127

Tickle Tune Typhoon Recordings
5731 31st NE
Seattle, Wash. 98105
206-524-9767

Time Warner
Sports Illustrated For Kids
P.O. Box 830606
Birmingham, Ala. 35282

Tomorrow River Music
P.O. Box 165
Madison, Wish. 53701
608-432-3095

Top Ten Software
40982 Highway 41
Oakhurst, Calif. 93644
209-683-7577

Tot
50 Fort Hill Rd.
Groton, Conn. 06340
203-448-67045

Touchstone
Buena Vista Home Video
500 South Buena Vista St.
Burbank, Calif. 91521-7145
800-72-DISNEY

Toys To Grow On
P.O. Box 17
Long Beach, Calif. 90801
800-542-8338

Tyke
2750 W. 35th St.
Chicago, Ill. 60632
800-533-8953

Uncle Milton Industries
3555 Hayden Ave.
Culver City, Calif. 90232-0246
310-559-1566

U.S. Games
179 Ludlow St.
Stamford, Conn. 06902-6912
203-353-8400

Video Presentations
2326 Sixth Ave. Ste. 230

Seattle, Wash. 98121
800-458-5335

Viking
375 Hudson St.
New York, N.Y. 10014
212-366-2000

Viking/Kestrel
(See above)

Voyager Company
1351 Pacific Coast Highway, Ste. 300
Santa Monica, Calif. 90401
213-451-1383

Walt Disney Computer Software
500 South Buena Vista St.
Burbank, CA 91521
818-841-3326

Warner Brothers
400 Warner Blvd.
Burbank, Calif. 91522
818-945-6000

Weekly Reader Software/
Optimum Resources
10 Station Pl.
Norfolk, Conn. 06058
800-327-1473

Western Publishing Co., Inc.
1220 Mound Ave.
Racine, WI 53404
800-558-3291

Wimmer-Ferguson
P.O. Box 10427
Denver, Colo. 80250
303-733-0848

WINGS for Learning
1600 Green Hills Rd.
P.O. Box 660002
Scots Valley, Calif. 95067-0002
800-321-7511

WonderWorks
4802 Fifth Ave.
New York, N.Y. 15213
800-262-8600

Woodstock Percussion
Box 381-A
West Hurley, N.Y. 12491
800-422-4463

World Folk Arts
115 Oaktree Pl.
Leonia, N.J. 07605
201-461-6137

Yellow Moon Press
P.O. Box 1316
Cambridge, Mass. 02238
617-628-7894

Young Naturalist Foundation
P.O. Box 11314
Des Moines, Iowa 50340
416-946-0406